An Introduction to the Study of African Culture

An Introduction to the Study of African Culture

SECOND EDITION

ERIC O. AYISI
Hampton Institute
Virginia, U.S.A.

London
HEINEMANN
Ibadan · Nairobi · Lusaka

Heinemann Educational Books Ltd
48 Charles Street, London W1X 8AH
P.M.B. 5205 Ibadan · P.O. Box 45314 Nairobi
P.O. Box 3966 Lusaka
EDINBURGH   MELBOURNE   AUCKLAND
TORONTO   HONG KONG   SINGAPORE
KUALA LUMPUR   NEW DELHI   KINGSTON

ISBN 0 435 89051 4
First published 1972
Second Edition 1979

Printed in Great Britain by
Fletcher & Son Ltd, Norwich

Contents

Dedicated to
DOROTHY
KATHLEEN
& RUTH

Foreword

DR AYISI must be congratulated on accomplishing a project that would have seemed impossible to most specialists on African culture and society. When he first told me about this book my curiosity was aroused on two sides. Take, to begin with, the idea of African culture: by what criteria can we include, under this rubric, both the culture of the Kung Bushmen of the Kalahari—those gentle, peaceful, propertyless, hunting and collecting folk who have been so aptly described as 'the harmless people' by Lorna Marshall—and the traditional patterns of life and thought of the sophisticated, materially wealthy, politically and socially complex, militarily organized kingdoms of West Africa—Ashanti and Benin, Yoruba and Hausa. Take next the idea of an 'introduction' to this vast panorama, so variegated in space and so marked by the chances and changes of history. Such an introduction, aimed presumably at the senior school leaver, the university entrant, and the general reader, would have to evoke interest and curiosity as well as provide instruction. In the idiom of today, it would have to be 'relevant' as well as academically sound. What themes and issues would one select for presentation? How would one retain a scholar's objectivity yet not avoid, or condone, or apologize for institutions and patterns of behaviour—whether traditional or of the colonial period or contemporary—that are repugnant to the modern mind?

Dr Ayisi has dealt neatly and boldly with these and the other problems that his undertaking must have presented him with. Reading his book, I am struck by his approach. It is, I think, essentially an African scholar's—perhaps, rather, an African educationist's approach. It appears in his crisp and compact style, as the spoken word does, so much more effectively than the written text, with the audience Dr Ayisi is aiming at. It is evident, also, in an unexpected feature of his exposition: why, one might ask, should an account of *African* kinship institutions include a quotation—well known to anthropologists—from an eighteenth-century classic on the Iroquois of North America, and a reference to L. H. Morgan, the founder of scientific kinship study? I venture to guess what Dr Ayisi's answer would be. Students of African societies must be made to understand that many of the traditional institutions and customs of these societies are not unique to Africa, but are local forms of types of institutions and customs found all over the world. They must learn to see Africa in a world perspective and in a framework of scholarly research while learning about Africa itself. Dr Ayisi keeps this consideration well to the fore. Introducing his readers to the essentials of African culture serves also to give them an outline of modern social anthropology.

However, what is of most interest is the choice of the topics Dr Ayisi has regarded as significant: the subjects of Sex and Marriage, Kinship, Household, and Lineage are obvious ones. There is ample material on these topics, and general principles of very wide application in Africa have been established and are clearly summarized by Dr Ayisi. The surprise comes with the chapters on Religion, Law, and Festivals. These topics, many would agree, concern matters of belief and practice that are more characteristically and specifically African than those dealt with in the earlier chapters, and it is far more difficult to generalize about them. Dr Ayisi solves this problem by drawing on his own experience and his field research among his own people in Ghana. It is a fortunate choice; for the peoples of Ghana are notable for the ways in which they have accommodated their basic traditional patterns of political, legal, and religious ideas and practices to the modern world, and this is regularly celebrated in the splendid socio-religious festivals in which the whole social order of a group is collectively acted out. In a sense Dr Ayisi is here dealing with ideal types, representative of African cultural patterns in their most developed form.

The book ends, appropriately, with a discussion of Social Change in Africa—in the colonial period, and since. Here, again, he relies largely on the Ghanaian experience. It is a useful model case for drawing attention not only to the negative aspects, but also to the positive contributions of the colonial era which have formed the basis of modern nationalist movements, and of the economic changes that underlie the general process of modernization in Africa. It is worth being reminded that the spread of Christianity and of Western education, and the emergence of modern forms of commerce and of the non-tribal national state under the leadership of new élites, have a long history preceding them and have not wholly wiped out traditional ways of life and value systems.

Dr Ayisi's book effectively fulfils its aims. It will meet an increasing desire among students in educational institutions as well as among the public at large to find out what are the characteristic features of African culture and how they have been adapted to the modern world.

MEYER FORTES
King's College
Cambridge

Preface

APART FROM natural factors which differentiate one individual from another or one tribal group from another or one racial stock from another racial stock, there is the cultural factor. The cultural factor is more marked and manifested in human beings than among animals. Biological or instinctual factors play a more important part in the personality development of animals than among human beings. For example it is difficult, almost impossible, to effect any change in a pig by attempting to keep it clean. Nor can any scientist attempt to make an elephant speak. A circus keeper can train monkeys and dogs to play a few tricks, but that is all.

Among human beings the biological factors may be modified and so it is possible to introduce new behaviour patterns into the personality development.

For example, biological differences like pigmentation of the skin may not tell us anything of an individual's personality except that the individual is black, brown or white skinned. An Afro-American may therefore have more in common with a white American than a Ghanaian though they may be biologically similar. An Italian and a Briton may have the same colour of skin with very slight colouring variation, but their behaviour patterns are different. We are told, however, by psychologists and sociologists that there are racial types, which are categorized by national characteristics, or stereotypes. Therefore in America, for example, certain racial groups are given stereotypes which set them apart from other groups. The Negro is said to be mentally inferior but endowed with superior and voluptuous, almost insatiable, sexual capacity. The Jew is said to be mercenary but intelligent, and so on. These stereotypes are used only to rationalize one ethnic group in its negative relationship with another. This ethnocentric attitude of one racial group against another, or one ethnic group against another, is not unique to American society.

It has been expressed in a variety of ways, and forms for many centuries. Sometimes foreigners regard the Continent of Africa as one vast homogeneous peoples, in the pre-Colonial era, only divided into many countries, by the European powers. Of course, this view is not substantiated by any valid historical facts, except by truncated and conjectural accounts.

The truth is colonialism rather merged certain warring ethnic groups together for administrative convenience under the Pax Britannica philosophy. In Ghana, for example, the Akans who are the largest ethnic group, regard themselves superior to the northerners, and the tribes of other ethnic groups. In its extreme form, ethnocentricism creates social aberration, and sometimes wars. The Nigerian Civil War had ethnocentric overtones, the Ibos against the Yorubas. It is an ancient human frailty, for even in the Middle Ages and in subsequent centuries, the nobility of Europe considered itself as having descended from a more superior ancestry. In France, for example, Count de Boulainvilliers declared proudly that there were only two races, the nobles whose ancestry could be traced to the Germanic conquerors, and the masses, who were descendants of the subject Celts and Romans. The most irrational type of ethnocentricism was exhibited in Hitler Germany. Under the ruse of salvaging from deterioration the Aryan race which was considered 'pure', Hitler mounted the most bestial fury, and hate against the Jews.

The philosophy of his atrocities were set out in his book ... *Mein Kampf*. 'If we divide the human race into three categories—founders, maintainers, and destroyers of culture—the Aryan stock alone can be considered as representing the first category.' (George Eaton Simpson and J. Milton Yinger, *Racial and Cultural Minorities: An Analysis of Prejudice and Discrimination*, 4th edition, Harper and Row Publishers, New York, p. 34, para. 4.)

These attempts to use race as paradigms for putting people in slots have failed, and it is becoming more and more clear, scientifically speaking, to use culture as the most important factor. In the last resort, culture is the most important factor in human development, and culture is manifested in many ways.

This book is a short and essentially simple introduction to African Studies. It is not a textbook of social anthropology, though it is hoped it will prove suitable for beginners in both sociology and anthropology. It is designed principally to meet the needs of first-year university students who are expected to take a course in African Studies.

I have included in the second impression two chapters, a prolegomenon, and a chapter on Pregnancy and Birth. In some areas I have made a few modifications, but the present book followed the format of the first. I have also borrowed many ideas from eminent social anthropologists, some of whom have been my teachers in both sociology and social anthropology. Professor Meyer Fortes inspired me both by his writings, and the fruitful academic association I have been privileged to enjoy with him for many years. The ideas herein expressed are familiar to many anthropologists, but I have tried to introduce new ideas in the simplest way possible.

It is hoped that this book will also be read by people who, though not students, are interested in African culture and history in general. Most of the examples I have used to illustrate the themes are taken from Ghanaian society.

I have provided a glossary of terms to assist newcomers to social anthropology, and a list of books for further reading.

Many people who helped me with the first book, I still feel indebted to them. Professor D. M. MacRae of the London School of Economics, my teacher and friend, from whom I gathered inspiration and intellectual stimulation, and to whom I owe more than I can express in my academic life; Professor Meyer Fortes for reading the manuscript and making useful corrections and suggestions; Professor J. H. Abraham, Head or former Head of the Sociology Department, University of Ghana, Legon; a friend, Mrs Eleanor Hill for helping me with the manuscript of the additional charters; Mrs Shirley Sherman for correcting a few stylistic mistakes for me, and Mrs Robin Disney for typing all the corrections.

Ramapo College of New Jersey
Gatehouse. Mahwah, N.J. Summer 1977

Prolegomenon

to the Introduction to the Study of African Culture

WHEN I thought of writing about African culture, I did not have any idea I would end up writing an introductory book on African Culture. The Institute of African Studies at the University of Ghana had arranged with Heinemann Educational Books to prepare a book of essays for courses offered by the Institute to the three Universities of Ghana. I was asked to write an article entitled 'Patterns of African Culture'. Instituted by a presidential order, these courses were mandatory for all students as part of projecting the African personality in the total education system of the country. 'African Genius' ... spelt out the philosophy behind the establishment of the Institute. The objectives, among others, are to research into the African past, to serve as a forum or meeting-place for scholars in African history and to teach courses reflecting the changing mood of the African spirit for freedom from the colonial rule. The African Genius:

What sort of African studies does Ghana want and need to have? In what way can Ghana make its specific contribution to the advancement of knowledge about the peoples and cultures of Africa through past history and through contemporary problems? For what kind of service are we preparing students of this Institute and our Universities to be identified with the aspirations of Ghana and Africa?

First and foremost, I would like to emphasize the need for a reinterpretation and assessment of the factors which make up the past. We have to recognize frankly that African studies, in the form in which they have been developed in the universities and centers of higher learning in the West have been largely influenced by the concepts of old style colonial studies and still to some extent to the colonial ideologies and mentality.

Until recently the study of African history was regarded as minor and marginal theme within the framework of imperial history. The study of social institutions and cultures was subordinated in varying degrees to the effort to maintain the apparatus of colonial power. In the British institutions of higher learning, for example, there was the tendency to look to social anthropologists to provide the kind of knowledge that would help to support their particular brand of colonial government known as indirect rule. The study of African languages was closely related to the practical objectives of the European missionaries and administrators. African music, dancing and sculpture were labelled 'primitive'. They were something grotesque, as curious, mysterious human backwater, which helped to retard social progress in Africa and to prolong colonial domination over its people.[1]

The above observations may be true in many ways, but the facts are grossly exaggerated. By the turn of the latter part of the eighteenth century a plethora of information about cultures of non-Western peoples were available to scholars. These data were made up of stories told by sailors, accounts of missionaries to these countries, and also accounts about the savage American Indians. The scholars at the time were ignorant of the meanings behind these cultures, and the best they could do was to view these cultures in Western epistemological contexts and categories.

For example, J. F. Lafitau wrote about the American Indians, and Martin Dobrizhoffer about the Abipones of South America. John Locke's systematic descriptions of cultures of different peoples are illuminating and they underscore the point I am trying to make. John Locke (1632–1704):

Had you or I been born at the Bay of Soldania, possibly our thoughts and notions had not exceeded those brutish ones of the Hottentots that inhabit there. And had the Virginia King Apochancana been educated in England, he had been perhaps as knowing a divine, as a good a mathematician as any in it, the difference between him a more improved Englishman lying barely in this, that the exercise of his faculties was bounded within ways, modes, and notions of his own country, and never directed to any other inquiries ... (Quoted in J. S. Slotkin, (ed.), *Readings In Early Anthropology*. Viking Fund Publications in Anthropology No. 40. Chicago Aldine Publishing Co., 1965, p. 173.)[2]

It is obvious that Locke was not down-grading these non-Western cultures, but he felt that they were not rational because they were not governed by the canons of systematic logic. These writers were trying to satisfy their intellectual curiosities, and also to make some meaning of these cultures, which were exotic and bizarre, quite different from what they had been used to in their various cultures.

For example, Jean-Jacques Rousseau (1712–78) being disenchanted with the social conditions of his time, romanticized about the past. His 'noble savages' were the Carib Indians of Venezuela whose ways of life he described with intense nostalgia. In his *Discourse on the Origin and Foundation of Inequality among Mankind* (1755), Rousseau ... postulated the early conditions of mankind as being a state of constant harmony as like an Elysian Universe, here people were organized in small groups, without laws or any other 'social constraints'. Life was simple, free from avarice and competition, not knowing the value of money. People lived by 'their emotions', and thus achieving a simple and a happy life that civilization has since destroyed ... The social life of the 'natural man', however, had little survival value because man was physically inferior to ferocious animals. He differed from them in that he possessed the faculty of improvement, so that he did not have to abide by the laws of nature. Eventually concepts of family life, property, government, law, and mutual cooperation were developed. While these institutions made his existence more viable, they also destroyed freedom and happiness ... (Annemarie de Wall Maefijt, *Images of Man: A History of Anthropological Thought*, Alfred A. Knopf, New York, 1974, p. 96.)

Rousseau, like Locke, was curious about the early conditions of the Western man and he regarded non-Western cultures as the early conditions of man. While Hobbes, the eighteenth-century social thinker, regarded these cultures as a 'state of nature—brutish' trammelled by internecine warfare, Rousseau extolled these cultures and spoke about them in glowing terms—'The Noble Savage', 'born free'. Rousseau, like Sigmund Freud, believed that man was basically good, only debased by civilization. (*Civilization and Its Discontents*. Hogarth, London, 1930.)

This debate about the early conditions of man, in relation to the non-Western cultures, continued well into the nineteenth century. Consequently, two schools of thought emerged both in England and France. One was the romanticism of Rousseau which followed the evolutionary line of thought, and the other the Biblical view of man's fall. The latter was led by Comte Joseph de Maistre (1753–1821). He attacked Rousseau's romantic view and suggested an alternative view to illustrate non-Western cultures ... This view, of course, was consistent with religious orthodoxy of the time ...

> Savage races came later than civilized races and represent their disintegration. One thing is sure, the savage is necessarily later in time than civilized man. For example, let us examine America. This country has every characteristic of a new land. But since civilization is of great antiquity in the old countries, it follows that the savages who inhabited America at the time of the discovery descended from man.[3]

While these debates were raging, the evolutionary theory had now become a respectable conceptual scheme by which reality was being explored in all areas of intellectual endeavour. Edward Tylor became fascinated by the evolutionary theory and he very quickly applied it to the study of culture. Incidentally, Tylor introduced the concept of 'Culture' into anthropology. According to Tylor, culture was analogous to natural organism. Since every organism evolved or developed in a uniform progressive manner, culture also followed this unlineal process. The corollary was that all human societies passed through the same series of stages ... 'Culture evolved from simple to complex and that all societies passed through barbarism to civilization.' (*Cultural Anthropology*, 2nd edition, Prentice-Hall Inc./Cliff, N. J., 1973.) Tylor represented the tradition of English thought at the time.

People of non-Western cultures were considered to be at a lower level of development which the Western world had already gone through. This pompous spirit of the mid-Victorian period was born of complacency and ignorance. Prosperity and expansion of trade were regarded as signs of being the 'elect' of God, charged with the responsibility of saving humanity from degeneration ...

> The spirit of progress no less than the surpluses and shortages
> of the industrial community drove Britons outward. Expansion
> was not simply a necessity without which industrial growth
> might cease, but a moral duty to the rest of humanity. In the
> Utilitarian science of political economy, the earlier Victorians
> beheld the rules for improvement everywhere. They were not the
> first, nor were they the last people to project their own image
> as universal ideal, nor mistake fortunate trends of national
> history for natural laws and bend foreigners to obey them. This
> was the authentic mid-Victorian outlook on the world. It was
> suffused with vivid sense of superiority and self-righteousness if
> with every good intention. Upon the ladder of progress, nations
> and races seemed to be higher or lower according to proven
> capacity of each for freedom and enterprise. The British at the top,
> followed, a few rungs below, by the Americans and other
> 'striving-go-ahead' Anglo-Saxons. The Latin peoples were
> thought to come next, though far behind. Much lower stood the
> vast oriental communities of Asia and North Africa where
> progress appeared to be crushed for centuries by military
> despotisms or smothered under passive religion. Lowest of
> all stood the 'aborigines'.

It was quite obvious that some of these writers were making honest mistakes in regard to their views about the non-Western cultures. Unless we would like to make superhumans of the white race, and believe that they were infallible and omniscient, and never made mistakes, then we should view their writings with subjective understanding, or in the Weberian term, *verstehen*.

It is part of the fraility of humanity to be speculative sometimes, when there is some doubt about our knowledge of a phenomenon or a fact. These men were endeavouring to find answers to certain philosophical and epistemological problems about the origins of cultures or civil societies.

By the turn of the twentieth century, the increase in knowledge of non-Western cultures, and the refinement of analytical tools in the social sciences radically changed the direction of the quest for knowledge and the interpretation of social phenomena.

Professor Jack Goody of Cambridge University and an undisputed scholar in the field of modern social anthropology, sets the historical record straight when he says *inter alia*:

'Both sociology and anthropology have grown out of the attempts of man to make sense of his social environment, the behaviour of his fellow men, the variations between different societies and changes that have taken place over time. In the Greek world, Aristotle examined some 150 possible constitutions, in the prolegomena to the history of the Berbers, the Arabic writer, Ibn Khaldun (1332–82), worked out a general theory of social development; in China Ma Tuan-Lin produced a comprehensive study of civilization (1320), in Europe, Montesquieu classified and compared the range of human societies in the Spirit of the Laws (1784). While Vico concerned himself, in the Science Nuova (1725) with examining the cycle of man's spiritual development in history. In the nineteenth century the task was pursued not only by sociological precursors, like Comte and Spencer, but also by a number of writers who specialized in the institutions of simpler societies.

The information about remote lands resulted from colonial expansion and subsequently incorporated into studies of human behaviour. Men like Waitz, Morgan, and Frazer attempted to discern general similarities in social action, physical, verbal and speculative of different societies.' (Jack Goody, *Comparative Studies in Kinship*. Routledge & Kegan Paul Ltd., London, 1969, p. 1.)

Goody sums up his analysis by combining the synchronic, and the diachronic approach in a complementary filiation with good effect. The accent, however, is on the diachronic, but this is uniquely Goody's style.

It is fair to say that Sir James Frazer (1854–1941) was the last of the writers who attempted to seek for universal laws and general similarities in human behaviour. Franz Boas with his theory of 'historical particularism' separates the two types of schools, that which ended at the early part of the twentieth century which he described as *nomothetic* approach, which aimed at discovering general laws or regularities, and the type which he himself believed in, known as the *idiographic* approach, which concerned itself with studying about a particular culture in all of its 'minutiae'.

Frazer is regarded in the English-speaking world, especially outside of the United States, as the founding father of modern anthropology. Many eminent British anthropologists can trace descent either directly or through a descendant to him. His influence was enormous during his lifetime. His *magnum opus, The Golden Bough*, was widely read, and it made converts of many scholars. For example, Malinowski was attracted to anthropology after he had read *The Golden Bough*. Sir Edmund Leach, a direct descendant of Frazer by way of Malinowski, now 'naturalized descendant' of Claude Levi-Strauss, the structuralist exponent in anthropology says of Frazer in contrast to his 'hero':

'Claude Levi-Strauss, Professor of social anthropology at the College de France, is, by common consent, the most distinguished exponent of this academic trade to be found anywhere outside the English-speaking world, but scholars who call themselves social anthropologists are of two kinds. The proto-type of the first was Sir James Frazer (1854–1941), author of *The Golden Bough*. He was a man of monumental learning who had no first-hand acquaintances with the lives of the primitive peoples about whom he wrote. He hoped to discover fundamental truths about the nature of human psychology by comparing the details of human nature on world-scale . . .'
(*Claude Levi-Strauss*, revised edition by Edmund Leach, edited by Frank Kermode. Modern Masters, The Viking Press, New York, 1974, p. 1.)

Frazer's influence was far-reaching, but this waned when the conceptual framework within which he wrote fell into disrepute. At the time Frazer began his writing the evolutionary approach was popular and respectable. His work was based on the evolutionary theory. *The Golden Bough* contained analyses of religious practices of simpler peoples. His insights were illuminating at the time he wrote, but now newer insights have eclipsed his ideas. Sir Edmund Leach continues his observations of these two great men in anthropology.

'The proto-type of the second was Bronislaw Malinowski (1884–1942), born in Poland but naturalized an Englishman, who spent most of his academic life analyzing the results of research which he himself had personally conducted over a period of four years in a single small village in far off Maelanesia. His aim was to show how this exotic community "functioned" as a social system and how its individual members passed through their lives from cradle to grave. He was more interested in the difference between human cultures than their over-all similarity ... Most of those who at present call themselves social anthropologists in either Britain or the United States claim to be "functionalists". Broadly speaking, they are anthropologists in the style and tradition of Malinowski.

In his day Malinowski had three kinds of celebrity. His renown among the general public was a prophet of free love. Though tame by modern standards, his accounts of the sexual eccentricities of the Trobriand Islanders were rated as near pornography. The almost passionate enthusiasm of professional colleagues rested on other grounds, first the novelty of his methods of field research which has now been universally imitated; second, the dogmas of his special brand of "functionalism" an oversimplified, mechanistic style of sociological theorizing are now genarally viewed with contempt.' (*Claude Levi-Strauss*, revised edition by Edmund Leach, edited by Frank Kermonde. Modern Masters, The Viking Press, New York, 1974, p. 1.)

Other admirers of Frazer and Malinowski pay them tributes with feelings of appreciation, and in the case of Malinowski with 'filial piety'. For example, Sir Raymond Firth says of Malinowski, in the collection of essays by former students:

'If he had lived for another decade, his dialectical skill, let
alone the richness of his creative mind, would have found
many answers to his critics and derived profit from their comment.
Much of this comment has been justified, but by no means
all, and sometimes his work has been passed over where credit
was due. Three factors in particular seem to be responsible for
this. One is that the climate of opinion, particularly in British
social anthropology, changed radically in the decade and half
after Malinowski left England. This was partly due to the
influence of Radcliffe-Brown and partly due to the growing
realization of the need for clearer structural approach, to give
more precision to many anthropological generations.'[4]

In spite of these apparent differences between these two scholars,
they both were responsible for laying firm foundations for British
anthropology. Malinowski's creative mind, and his sensitivity to
social phenomena, enabled him to disentangle the intricate social
fabric and make sense of it. Radcliffe-Brown's mental alertness and
probity of his research techniques enabled him to unravel meanings
hidden in the proclivities of the social structure of simple societies . . .
Malinowski, like Franz Boas, did not 'dignify' the nomothetic
approach. He had a passion for the idiographic approach. According to him, reconstructing the past 'by conjectural history'[5] was not
history and was the refuge of charlatans and dilettanti. If anthropology would command any intellectual respectability, then anthropologists should not conjecture; they should view the social systems
as scientists. Malinowksi's meticulous expertise in field research is
described by Professor Phyllis Kaberry in the following words:

'He gave ethnography a dimension it had hitherto lacked:
actuality of relationships, and richness of content. Instead of a
nondescript field where anonymous informants provided
genealogies, recounted their folk tales, stated the norms and
apparently conformed to them, we become familiar with the
Trobriands and its shaded villages, the changing aspects of
its garden through seasons, its decorated canoes drawn up on
the beach or moored in the Kiriwiana lagoon. We come
to know the inhabitants, not as paid and perhaps bored

informants, but as actors in a changing scene, as individuals who cooperate, quarrel, cheat, compromise, give generously, contradict one another, and also Malinowski on occasion diverges from rules, pays the penalty, or sometimes avoids it. In short, we are always aware of the context of the situation in which Malinowski made his generalizations, and with him we trace the intricacies of multiple relationships. (Ibid., *Man and Culture*, Routledge & Kegan Paul Ltd.)

The first-generation students of Malinowski and Radcliffe-Brown were scholars of enormous intellectual statures. Raymond Firth (now Sir Raymond Firth), an economist from New Zealand; Meyer Fortes from South Africa, with keen sensitivity to philosophical and abstract concepts; Audrey Richards, a graduate from Cambridge University; Edmund Leach; Jomo Kenyatta; and many others. They were sent to 'colonize' the world of non-Western cultures, to examine their cultures and bring back whatever they saw of these peoples. Firth to Tikopians, Fortes to the Ashantis and the Tallensi, Lucy Mair, and Audrey Richards to East Africa, and Gluckman and Schepera to South Africa, Nadel to the Nupe, Leach to India, and Jomo Kenyatta to learn of his own tribe, the Kikuyu.

Except for Kenyatta, who was a special case, these scholars, 'besides being representatives of the "colonial nation", a manifestation of "white power", their presence among these peoples was no cause of offence. They had access to every information and they were treated as scholars from the city designing to live among the people. It was his status as an elevated stranger, a friendly conqueror that enabled him to walk almost into any house, to ask any question, to attend almost any ceremony, public or private ...' (*Comparative Studies of Kinship.*)

These scholars built a new corpus of anthropological knowledge, gave it the intellectual respectability and academic recognition that the British have been enjoying for decades. British anthropology rests either on the functional or structural–functional approach. The anthropologist engages in the study of the total social system of a society; in other words, social structure. The components of the social structure are said to be the network of social behaviour, and these are social relationships articulated in the social institutions.

Social institutions are defined by their social functions, religious, magical, legal, economic, etc.

Most anthropologists remain entrenched in the structural–functional orthodoxy at the complete neglect of historical data. But some anthropologists endeavour to use, where possible, some historical data, in order to put their analysis into sharp perspectives. For example, Fortes in his work among the Ashanti, and the Tallensi in Northern Ghana adopted the structural–functional approach to good effect. Fortes used kinship as the main paradigm of his social investigations among these two societies. He agreed with other writers that kinship ties are the mnemonics of the total social field of every society, and that certain societies seem to emphasize the ties in the maternal line more than those in the paternal line. The concept of unilineality derived from this opposing category is matrilineal/patrilineal. He found that the biological and sociological distinctions which other writers had pointed out were plausible. For example he agreed with Rattray, who had previously studied the Ashantis and written voluminously about the various aspects of the people. He, however, maintained that this distinction was a matter of degree. From his personal observations, he concluded that both sides of the family were equally important, in specific ways. Forde had previously found this inconsistency in the kinship structure of the Yako in Eastern Nigeria. He had described this web of kinship system by the term 'double-descent'. Fortes did not find this concept suitable for the kinship structure of the societies he studied.

He realized that Malinowski's dichotomy of biological/sociological paternity implied that the child's father in a matrilineal society becomes the affine, a stranger with no jural obligation for or over the child. He only exercised rights in *genitricem* over the mother, provided food for the mother of the child, and also the necessary semen for procreation (natural insemination as opposed to artificial insemination). This superficial analysis of the real social situation was not acceptable to Fortes. Fortes is always a few decades ahead of some of his professional colleagues. When the unilineality had taken firm root in structural analysis in anthropology, he very quickly detected the apparent incongruity in the concept. He realized that Forde's 'double-descent' was a unique phenomenon, and could not take care of his concern. He therefore created a new concept 'complementary filiation'. This concept, 'complementary filiation' provided full articulation to the dogma of ties between a child and his parents, while at the same time explains the rationale for a stress on either the maternal or paternal ties because of *inherent de jure* customary practices.

Sir Edmund Leach, in his *Rethinking Anthropology*, said of this concept as follows:

'Professor Fortes has devised a special concept "complementary filiation" which helps him to describe this double unilineal element in Tallensi/Ashanti pattern while rejecting the notion that societies actually possess unilineal systems (Fortes, 1953, p. 33, 1959). It is interesting to note the circumstances which led to the development of this concept. From one point of view, "complementary filiation" is simply an inverse form of Malinowski's notion of "sociological paternity" applied in the matrilineal context of the Trobrian society. But Fortes has done more than invent a new name for an old idea; he has made the cornerstone of a substantial body theory, and the theory arises logically from the circumstances of his own field experience.'

Fortes has contributed in a large measure towards the development of the anthropological theory, as these are found in most of his writings. He has provided fresh insights into religion 'Job and Oedipus', broader perspective of the function of kinship ties, and many topics. He represents the rich tradition of British scholarship, and prolific writings. In some cases all the facts were not visible to him; therefore, his conclusions may not be comprehensive, or definitive. But hindsight is more enlightened than foresight, and if there are any gaps in some of his writings, the situation may have changed since he wrote, or other intervening variables have affected these conclusions.

Fortes and his contemporaries were true scholars, never court-scholars providing knowledge to prolong colonial domination.

It has been necessary to write the preceding history about the development of social anthropology, since its subject-matter is culture. If the reader finds that my writings reflect British orientations, I would plead with him to be patient with me, and read this book with the idea that this impression is deliberate; I hold it as an inconvertible truth, that no African writer can depart from the corpus of knowledge which Western writers have gathered together, and organized in the conceptual frame of reference, and produce any work that will command any intellectual respectability. We find ourselves in a new era, an era of filling the gaps in our history, which are necessary if we hope to serve posterity.

The *obiter dictum* of the greatest of all teachers should be our policy: 'I come not to destroy the laws and the prophecy, I come to fulfill.'

REFERENCES

1 African Genius: An opening address at the opening of the Institute of African Studies. (Ghana Government Publication, 1960.)

2 Victor Barnoun, *Introduction to Anthropology*, revised edition, The Dorsey Press, 1971–72, p. 18.

3 Victor Barnoun, *Introduction to Anthropology*, revised edition, p. 20, para. 4.

4 *Man and Culture: An Evaluation of Malinowski*, Routledge & Kegan Ltd.

5 The term *conjectural history* was created by Radcliffe-Brown.

I

What is Culture?

———————————◆———————————

SINCE MAN first inhabited this planet, it has been one long struggle
for survival between himself and nature. Man has had to live and
also to find his place in the universe. In the process man has left
behind traces of his achievements at various levels of his development, and the cumulative knowledge of his various achievements
constitutes what we refer to as culture. We are told that man has
evolved from very primitive origins and has made a staggering
jump to the present stage.

According to Piddington:

> The culture of a people may be defined as the sum total
> of the material and intellectual equipment whereby they
> satisfy their biological and social needs and adapt
> themselves to their environment.[1]

Piddington's definition spells out what I have said—that man has
to struggle for survival and also reconcile himself to nature.

But there are other definitions of culture, and it is worthwhile
for us to look at them. Malinowski's own definition (quoted from
Tylor):

> Culture is that complex whole which includes knowledge,
> belief, art, law, morals, customs, and all other capabilities
> and habits acquired by man as a member of society.[2]

Tylor is here distinguishing between the instinctive qualities of
man and his acquired qualities. Malinowski made use of some of
the Tylorian items of culture; he maintained that culture comprises inherited artefacts, goods, technical processes, ideas, habits
and values.[3] As Dr Audrey I. Richards points out:

> A term such as 'culture' and 'structure' as used in sociological

work, is inevitably a heuristic device or a way of looking
at facts and hence the meaning can best be grasped by a
study of its use in the analysis of the data.

Malinowski used the term to cover both man's sociological and
biological needs, and the way these needs have been met by organized procedural arrangements. Malinowski's concept of culture is
consistent with his views on primitive societies which he demonstrated in his various monographs and major anthropological contributions. His conceptual framework was neatly incorporated in
the notions of charter and the structural-functional analysis of social
facts.

Culture, then, embraces everything which contributes to the
survival of man, and this will comprise not only physical factors
but also sociological factors. A distinction has been made between
our biological and social needs. The psychological factors will
comprise all the non-material interests such as religious institutions,
ritual observances, etc.

In order to understand the basic principles on which human
society functions, we must know something about the institutions
of the society. Human beings, in order to live normal lives in
reasonable peace must behave in prescribed ways. These ways of
behaving are acquired during the period of socialization, and
education, and through experience. They are so institutionalized
that they have become part of our social systems. Though we are
aware of them, they are outside the individual, and they have the
power of coercion over him. Emile Durkheim referred to these
ways of behaving as 'social facts' or 'collective manifestations'.
Social facts, then, constitute the various institutions which guide
and direct our actions in society.

Culture comprises the way of behaving; it is the way we do
things. Another aspect of culture is, therefore, the means by which
we do things. Implements, artefacts, paintings, figurines for religious observances, and all the integrative forces such as religion
are elements of culture. Ecological factors influence human behaviour; therefore cultures have a symbiotic affinity with their
environments, including geographical factors.

As there are many and varied environments, there are also many
and varied cultures. The English kiss loved ones: a man may kiss

2

a lady on the cheek as a symbol of affection or on the lips with deep passion if they are lovers. The continental Europeans do something quite different—men kiss their fellow men on both cheeks. The Ghanaian who has never lived in either of these cultures would consider men kissing their fellow men as ridiculous and feeble, although chiefs may embrace distinguished guests as a sign of cordiality and welcome. When a man behaves in a way considered to be feminine in Ghana, it is said to be odd, and the only explanation given to this behaviour is that the man is impotent. The English gentleman gets up for a lady, but the Ghanaian lady, unless she is westernized, gets up for a man. All these various ways of behaving are part of culture. The term culture is thus an imprecise way of describing the social realities in any given society.

Lucy Mair described one view of culture as follows:

This definition—which is really an enumeration—has sometimes been compressed into the statement that Culture comprises all kinds of learned behaviour and in practice the distinguishing feature of the study of culture is often said to be that it is concerned with 'art', 'customs', and 'ways'. By 'art' Tylor meant techniques and because some leading students of culture such as Boas in America have been concerned with the collection of specimens for museums, the objects which the techniques create are often called 'material culture'. A culture then is the common possession of a body of people who share the same traditions in social terms. Such a body is a society.[4]

We have so far been going round in circles repeating things others have already said about culture. But as Audrey Richards has said, the term culture is a heuristic device which serves as a conceptual tool for indicating certain features of the important landmarks in the social field, so that certain activities and certain objects may have a meaningful existence in the social system.

The term culture has acquired other meanings besides those given to it by sociologists. Semantically the term may have some emotive quality. We hear of people being described as cultured or uncultured. This refers to whether or not a person is socially adjusted or refined or civilized or is a cultural deviant or a misfit.

3

These ways of looking at culture differ from the so-called 'scientific' approach.

We may, however, use the term as defined by the writers referred to previously and try to define the structure of African culture. This enterprise will lead us to looking closely at certain social realities of African society.

But first, we should clarify one more confusion. The culture of a place is sometimes said to be indigenous, implying that it is exclusive and peculiar to that society, but this is invalid because of cultural contact or acculturation. There is no culture that could be said to be pure. For example, Roman and Greek cultures have influenced other European cultures in many ways. Most African cultures have been influenced by Western culture and linguists tell us that names of certain African foods are either Portuguese, Danish, or Dutch. *Panoo*, the Akan word for bread, we are told is Portuguese, and so on. This difficulty is circumvented by the use of the term 'traditional' to imply the pure culture of a place. For the term traditional applied to government or dancing implies the indigenous government or dancing of that part of Africa. Anthropologists are concerned with such things as conventions, customs, and the material objects that are the main items that keep a society going. We can therefore treat culture as part and parcel of every society. Culture consists of the ways, mores and beliefs transmitted from generation to generation; it may be generally shared by some population or a group of people—in other words, it should represent the *collective conscience* of a group of people. If culture is not generally accepted by all the members of the group, and it does not fit neatly into the normative system of a group, then it cannot be considered culture.

Sometimes cultural traits are articulated in collective manifestations or racial idiosyncrasies and pecularities.

Culture must also be learned through socialization. The differences in culture derive from several factors; among them are race, ethnicity, climate, etc.

We can therefore treat culture as part and of every society. What is a society? Society is made up of the aggregate of groups of people and the basic unit of any society is the family. The family is formed by the union of a man and woman and children—by the institution

4

known as marriage. I shall, therefore, discuss the question of sex and marriage in the next chapter.

REFERENCES

1 R. Piddington, *Introduction to Social Anthropology*, London: Oliver & Boyd, 1950, p. 3.

2 Raymond Firth (ed.), *Man and culture: An evaluation of the work of Bronislav Malinowski*, London: Routledge & Kegan Paul Ltd., 1957, p. 16.

3 Firth (ed.), 1957. *Man and Culture: The Concept of Culture in Malinowski's Work*, p. 15.

4 Lucy Mair, *An Introduction to Social Anthropology*, Oxford: The Clarendon Press, 1965, pp. 7–8.

II

Sex and Marriage

EVERY SOCIETY has certain rules which regulate sexual practices. Some African societies regard sex as the most important factor in marriage and therefore a premium is placed on virginity. Girls on marriage are expected to be virgins and are rewarded accordingly. Among the Akans, mothers are presented with gifts by sons-in-law if at the first intercourse with a bride the girl bleeds and soils the bed. This is indicative of the girl's virginity. But these cases are rare today because pre-marital sexual congress is not frowned upon in many African societies. What is prohibited is sexual intercourse before rite-de-passage or initiation for girls; among the Kipsigis of Kenya such sexual intercourse resulting in pregnancy is regarded as sacrilegious.[1] So it is not surprising that among the Kipsigis of Kenya, the offence of making an uninitiated girl pregnant is one of the most heinous that can be committed, and the girl and her child in the past used to be cast out of the community.

Besides this sexual prohibition, sexual intercourse is not permitted between near kin and is referred to as being incestuous; there are rules which prescribe and regulate the social area within which sexual intercourse is regarded as incestuous. The rules of incest prohibition enjoin people to marry outside their kin group and marriage thus contracted is referred to as *exogamy*. The rules of incest and *exogamy* are therefore complementary. The relationships within which sexual intercourse is not permitted or is considered incestuous are those of parent and child or brother and sister. Lucy Mair describes the Western system in her book:

In Western culture, incest is thought of as something particularly dreadful, not to be mentioned without a shudder, if at all. We have all heard of Oedipus, who was so appalled when he learned that he had unknowingly married his mother that he put out his eyes. The Elizabethan dramatists liked to ascribe incestuous relations to particularly villainous characters.[2]

There are, however, exceptions to the rule of *exogamy*, for in some situations in-group marriages are encouraged. These are desirable in certain societies, but in others are the rule, deviation from which is condemned. Marrying within a specified group (*endogamy*) is common among the caste-structured groups such as Indians and religious bodies such as the Catholics. At other times, too, where *exogamy* is practised, certain forms of marriage are encouraged such as cross-cousin marriage and preferential marriage.

Nowadays many societies are becoming permissive and sexual intercourse is not treated as a dark secret. We read of the hippies and 'flower boys and girls' in England and the United States and the sex life of undergraduate students all over the world. Sex is being brought into the open. Society is recognizing the facts of life and it is only sex education that will give sex its rightful place in the society. Though the modern trend in sexual activity gives the impression that society will soon slip into a jungle of promiscuity, this is not true, for most people treat sex with respect.

Marriage is an institution which is common to all human societies.[3] The theory that marriage was an advanced form of a union between man and woman and that in primitive societies promiscuity prevailed, has been disproved by anthropological writings. Westermarck was the first to state that marriage was part of human culture. Marriage is therefore the means by which a man and a woman come together to form a union for the purpose of procreation. African marriages are effected for just this purpose and therefore a childless marriage ceases to be meaningful in this context. For every marriage to be legal, certain requirements have to be fulfilled, and it should be preceded by certain customary observances.

In most African societies all unions between a man and a woman are regularized by the exchange of gifts and payments in kind by the man's people to the bride's people. These goods or payments are called *prestations* and they vary from one society to another.[4] They confer certain rights and duties on the partners of the union, viz. *rights in personam*. These are personal rights which are reciprocal obligations on two people in the performance of certain

7

duties: Thus in relation to the legal status established between an African husband and his wife, each partner has to perform specific duties to the other. These rights then form the legal basis of all customarily recognized marriages.

There are various forms of marriage. The *monogamous* form consists of a man, his wife and children, but a *polygamous*[5] marriage means that either the wife or husband has more than one spouse. If the husband has two or more wives, it is termed *polygyny*. The much less common form of a wife having more than one husband is called *polyandry*. There is also the marriage known as the *levirate*[6] that is a man inheriting his brother's widow. Sometimes a woman may marry the widow of a deceased brother and then permit a member of her lineage or 'family' to co-habit with the woman. Children of such a union belong to the woman who is the 'husband' of the widow. This is consistent with the dogma of African paternity. Anthropologists distinguish between biological and sociological paternity.

There are three important aspects of marriage which are of great social significance. First, marriage involves some modification or rupture of relations between the bride and her immediate kin. This is less noticeable if the future husband comes to live with and work for his parents-in-law. This rule, which requires a man to go and live with his wife's people is referred to as *matrilocal*, but other anthropologists choose to call it by another term, *uxorilocal*, meaning to live with the wife's people. Sometimes the rupture is more marked if the wife has to go and live with the future husband's people—*patrilocal* or *virilocal* as others prefer to call it; or *neolocal* when the partners elect to live on their own. Other anthropologists prefer to describe the rule which requires a man to go to live with his wife's people as *avunculocal*, meaning that the wife's children and the man live with the wife's brother. Here the referential point is the children.

The second aspect of marriage is that it confers certain rights on the wife and corresponding duties on the husband and *vice versa*. The various rights that a man acquires after he has performed all the necessary customs (prestations) are divided into two classes. They are, firstly, *rights in uxorem*, meaning rights over a woman as a sexual and domestic partner, and secondly, *rights in genetricem*, which are the rights of a woman as a mother. This means that

8

the man has to feed and protect the wife and children.[7]

In most African societies, if someone commits adultery with the woman, the man has to claim compensation which is known in Akan as *ayefare* or adultery fee. If this intercourse produces a child, the child belongs to the husband because the Akans say that 'Owifo nni ba',—'A thief has no child'. Depending on the society, the father may have certain rights over the children—this is referred to as a *jural right*. If the society is matrilineal, then the jural right is invested in the wife and the wife's people. The right which the father acquires over the children in a patrilineal society is referred to as *patria potestas*, and in a matrilineal society as *matria potestas*.

The third aspect is that marriage is not between a man and a woman, i.e. the immediate partners, but between families. This being the case, the kinsmen of both parties have a lively interest in the union. Since everyone becomes involved in marriage, certain rules have to be observed in order to maintain the solidarity of the relationship which has been created by a marriage between two persons and the relatives of the immediate partners and which is called *affinity*—the people become affines. Special rules of conduct are expected between affines and in some cases a discreet social distance is maintained. Anthropologists have shown interest in the custom found in many parts of Africa which is commonly known as 'mother-in-law avoidance'. This custom requires that social distance should be maintained between a husband and his wife's mother, and in extreme cases social contact is prohibited. This custom is explained by the fact that if social contact were encouraged between a man and his wife's mother there might be incestuous dealings between the two. According to Radcliffe-Brown:

> What is really the same custom varies from complete or nearly complete avoidance to the maintenance of social distance by a reciprocal attitude of reserve and respect. Amongst the Ganda no man might see his mother-in-law or speak face-to-face with her. Amongst the Galla a man must not mention the name of his mother-in-law (actual or prospective) but he does not appear to be prohibited from speaking to her. But

he may not drink milk from a cup she has used nor eat food of her cooking.[8]

Thus the custom has many varied forms. In some societies it is confined to a man's own mother-in-law. In others a man must practise the same sort of avoidance towards the mother-in-law of his brother. In many societies there is similar avoidance of the sisters of the mother-in-law, and occasionally of the wife's grandmother. But a man must also avoid, or maintain a respectful distance from some of his wife's male relatives, particularly her father, sometimes her father's brothers and in some societies, the mother's brother.

It is said that amongst the Toro of Albert Nyanza, the avoidance between son-in-law and father-in-law is even more rigid than that between son-in-law and mother-in-law; amongst the Lendu, another tribe in Uganda, the father-in-law can never visit his son-in-law except in the event of the serious illness of his daughter, whereas the mother-in-law may visit her son-in-law and his wife when two months have passed since the marriage.

With this custom of maintaining social distance from one's affines on the wife's side goes another contrary custom known as 'joking relationship'. This custom is very common in Africa and North America:

Ethnographers had reported from North America, Oceania, and Africa, instances of a custom by which persons standing in certain relationships resulting either from kinship, or more usually from marriage, were permitted or required to behave towards one another in a disrespectful or insulting way at which no offence might be taken. Such relationships came to be called 'joking relationships', admittedly not a very good name. The most numerous and widespread examples of this custom were in the relationship of a man to the brothers and sisters of his wife. But it was also found in some instances between mother's brother and sister's son, and in a somewhat milder form between grandparents and grandchildren.[9]

This 'joking relationship' allows people to indulge in horseplay and outrageous behaviour towards people who are related to them by marriage. This point is succinctly stated by Lucy Mair:

Parties to such a relationship are allowed and expected to
behave towards one another in ways that would be considered
outrageous in every context. Insult and obscenity are
permitted and the victim is obliged to take it all in good
part.[10]

Marriage is necessary for the establishment of the formal family,
and I shall discuss this in the next chapter.

REFERENCES

1 Mair, 1965, p. 75.

2 Mair, 1965, p. 76.

3 *Notes and Queries in Anthropology*, Routledge and Kegan
Paul, London, 1960, p. 100. Sixth edition revised and rewritten by
a Committee of the Royal Anthropological Institute of Great
Britain and Ireland, Preface by Brenda Z. Seligman. 'Marriage is a
union between a man and a woman such that children born to the
woman are the recognized legitimate offspring of both partners.'
This means that when children are born outside marriage, unless
the union is formalized by completing customary marriage requirements, the paternity of the children is said to be putative, because
the biological fathers have no jural or legal claim over the children.

4 For example, *Tiri Nsa*, or head rum, among the Akans in
Ghana and *Lobola* in Southern Africa.

5 Mair, 1965, p. 82. 'Much the commonest form of polygamy is
the marriage of one man to a number of women; so much so that
this is what most people understand by the word polygamy, though
the pedantically correct term for it is polygyny. The marriage of a
woman to a number of men is polyandry'.

6 *Notes and Queries in Anthropology*, p. 117. 'Secondary marriage: The choice of secondary mates may be free, but certain
secondary marriages may be enjoined and are usually correlated
with the laws of inheritance and the status of widows. The most
common is that known as the levirate by which a man is bound to
marry his brother's widow. The type of marriage may be practised
in societies founded on either a patrilineal or matrilineal basis.'

7 Mair, 1965, p. 84.

8 A. R. Radcliffe-Brown, and C. Daryll Forde (eds.), *African Systems of Kinship and Marriage*, London: International African Institute, Oxford University Press, 1950, p. 55.

9 A. R. Radcliffe-Brown, *Structure and Function in Primitive Society*, London: Cohen and West, 1952, p. 105.

10 Mair, 1965, p. 91.

III

The Family

Lewis Henry Morgan attempted to trace the origin of the family, and in the process postulated a theory which is now viewed with contempt by many anthropologists, especially outside the Soviet Union. He contended that there was a necessary and close relationship between technological development and culturally different patterns. The corollary was that family, like civilization, which according to E. B. Tylor had evolved through three basic stages; savagery, barbarism, and civilization; the family too had gone through similar progressive stages.

The family, according to Morgan's theory, started as a 'horde living in promiscuity' with no sexual regulations and inhibitions, hence no real family life. Followed by incestuous relationships between brothers and sisters. (Brothers and sisters mating.)

The third stage was characterized by group marriage, but strict observance of the rules of incest prohibition, 'sexual commonwealth or communism'.

The fourth stage, which according to Morgan coincided with barbarism, was characterized by 'loosely paired male and female' but each individual could live with other people.

The fifth stage was the 'husband dominant family' in which the husband could have more than one wife or polygamous family. Finally the stage of civilization heralded monogamous family. This was an evolutionary approach, and, as fantastic as this was, Morgan was able to influence many people, and Marx and Engels incorporated this idea in the communist ideology about property and the family.

The evolutionary approach to the study of culture and social institutions is now in great disrepute, and the accepted method is that espoused by Malinowski and Radcliffe-Brown. To conjecture about the origin of the family does not help one to understand the structure of the family. After all one does need to know about the origin of his nose before knowing what the nose is used for, or either what it is made of before one can use it. I follow the structural–functional approach.

The functional approach is associated with the name of Bronislaw Malinowksi (1884–1942). Malinowski was a scientist originally but was attracted to anthropology after reading Sir James Frazer's *The Golden Bough*. Malinowski's theoretical orientation rests on the assumption that all cultural traits serve basic or derived needs of individuals in a society. In order to serve these needs individuals have to create certain strategies to realize their aims. The needs of individuals are, among others, nutrition, reproduction, bodily comfort, safety, relaxation, movement, and growth. According to Malinowski, in the process of meeting these basic needs, we generate secondary needs ...

> Some aspects of the culture satisfy these basic needs. In doing
> so, they give rise to derived needs that must also be satisfied by
> the culture. For example, culture traits that satisfy the basic
> need for food give rise to the secondary, or derived, need for
> cooperation in food collection or production. Hence societies
> will develop forms of political organization and social control
> that guarantees required cooperation.[1]

Radcliffe-Brown, one of the founding fathers of British anthropology, although agreeing with Malinowski's view, he extended the concept beyond the functional aspect.

Radcliffe-Brown (1881–1955) was the proponent of the structural–functionalist approach. He maintained that human social behaviour was the product of the cultural traits, in other words, various aspects of social behaviour exist to maintain a society's social structure, and not solely to satisfy individual needs. The social structure of a society is the total network of its existing social relationship.

An example of Radcliffe-Brown's structuralist approach is his analysis of how potential tension that may exist between in-laws are avoided by the mechanism of either a joking relationship or avoidance relationship. In the former instance affinal relationship is placed on humorous basis, and interactions are characterized by horse-play or banter. In the latter case, strict rules may be prescribed to forbid the persons involved in affinal ties to interact face-to-face. Both Malinowski's view and Radcliffe-Brown's are used in complementary conjunction. If reproduction is one of the basic needs of individuals, then the derived need is marriage, and it may be extrapolated that marriage is ideally for reproduction.

The Family is then the logical outcome of marriage. A family consists of a man, his wife, and child or children. By this definition, a childless marriage is not a family. An individual belongs to at least one family in his lifetime. Family into which he is born is a family of orientation and later when he marries he forms a new family—a family of procreation. In most African societies a man may lose his wife if it is believed that he is sterile or impotent. By and large the fecundity of men is taken for granted, but if a woman has had a child before a second marriage and if the current marriage is childless, then the cause of sterility is attributed to the man. The family is therefore the basic unit of every social group which is localized and bound together by biological and social ties. Professor Lucy Mair describes the family as a domestic unit in which parents and children live together.

There are various types of families, depending on the structure of each family. A man, his wife and child or children constitute a nuclear or elementary family. When this unit is called conjugal family, it means the husband–wife relationship is of primary importance.

Levi-Strauss used this concept in a special way to distinguish it from the universalistic view which treats the nuclear family as building-blocks of social structure. He contends that the most important aspect of the family is that it is founded upon the institution of marriage, and therefore it unites two kin groups in reciprocal obligations and mutual interests. He quotes the Trobriand Islanders among whom the bride's kin must provide the basic food for her family even though he lives with her husband and his kin. The conjugal family has certain autonomy but is 'commonly enmeshed in an extended kinship system'. Furthermore, kinsmen often exercise great control over the conjugal pair, and frequently dictate the choice of mate. The characteristics of the conjugal family are these:

(1) It finds its origin in marriage; (2) It consists of a husband, wife, and children born of their wedlock, though it can be conceived

that other relatives may find their place close to that nuclear group; (3) The family members are united by (*a*) a legal bond, (*b*) economic, religious, and other kinds of rights and obligations, (*c*) a precise network of sexual rights and prohibitions, and (*d*) varying and diversified feelings such as love, affection, respect, awe ...'[2]

Bottomore also makes the following pertinent point:

The individual nuclear family is a universal social phenomenon. As Lowie writes: 'It does not matter whether marital relations are permanent or temporary, whether there is polyandry or sexual license, whether conditions are complicated by the addition of members included in our family circle, the one fact stands out beyond all others that everywhere the husband, wife and immature children constitute a unit from the remainder of the community.[3]

A man, his wives and children make up a *compound family* because it is based on a polygynous marriage which is a complex legal marriage with a common man linking all the wives and the children. Professor Evans-Pritchard describes another form of family as a *natural family* when the family is not the result of marriage, the relationship being one of concubinage. The *extended family* is common to most African societies, and it forms the *raison d'être* of all social co-operations and responsibility. It acts as a social security for the members of the group. It is smaller than the lineage in span, but discreet. The extended family consists of a number of joint families, and a joint family is made up of heads of two or three lineally related kinsfolk of the same spouses and offspring, and who occupy a single homestead.[4]

'A group may be described as a joint family when two or more lineally related kinsfolk of the same sex, their spouses and offspring, occupy a single homestead and are jointly subject to the same authority or single head. The term extended family should be used for the dispersed form corresponding to a joint family'.

Another type of joint family common in Africa is the patrilineal extended family.

'What is sometimes called a patrilineal extended family is formed by a custom whereby sons remain in their father's family group, bringing their wives to live with them, so that their children also belong to the group. Among the Bemba of Northern Rhodesia there is found a matrilineally extended family, a domestic unit consisting of a man and his wife with their daughters and husbands and children of the latter. The groups break up and new groups of the same kind are formed when a man obtains permission to leave his parents-in-law taking his wife and children with him'.[5]

In addition there is what is referred to as *ghost marriage* which may result in a compound family because the family consists of the ghost pater, his wife, their children and the kinsman, who becomes the genitor after the death of his brother.

In all plural marriages, children may either belong to both parents or to one of the wives, but may have common paternity. Children who belong to both parents are full siblings. Full siblings are persons of either sex who have the same father and mother (brother—male sibling; sister—female sibling).

The above type of family is found in most African societies where there are children whose relationships are expressed not *semenally* alone but *uterinely*. If the rules of descent are patrilineally oriented, then all the children maintain enduring solidarity because their jural interests are invested in the father's people in matters of inheritance and succession. But if it is matrilineally oriented, the semenal ties are of less social significance because the children have different jural interests which are invested in the mother and mother's people. Agnatic ties are of temporary social significance in matrilineally structured societies.

Apart from the family, the smallest social group, there are other groups which are caused by the accretions of secondary kinship ties. These are the household and lineages and I want to say something briefly on kinship. The concept of kinship is crucial to the understanding of small-scale societies. Kinship is important, in fact, in all societies because it refers to blood relationships between individuals. It is used for describing relationships in a narrow sense as well as in a broader sense. Parents and their children are a kin group of a special kind and the relationship between parents is referred to as that of affinity. The relationship of the children to one another and to the parents is a blood relationship—one of consanguinity.

The social significance of kinship ties, however, covers a wider social field in most African societies than in Western societies. In Western culture, its significance does not extend beyond the nuclear family in the ordinary classes. It is only in the aristocracy that the 'blood flows through many veins' and even there it is sometimes restricted in matters of succession by the principle of primogeniture —direct succession instead of generational succession. The present Queen of England's heir is the Prince of Wales, not Princess Margaret. This means that although Princess Margaret's children and grand-children have some royal blood, they are not in the direct line of succession to the English throne. It is therefore necessary to re-define our term of kinship to mean that two individuals are kin to each other, either by birth, descent or marriage.

Fortes (1945) used this kinship concept to describe the Tale societies, bringing out in broad relief certain important facts about their family systems and the intricate fabric of their social structure. He also (1949) discussed the political structure of these people.[6] In another book jointly edited by Fortes and Evans-Pritchard, they observed that in one type of African society:

the largest political unit embraces a group of people all of whom are united to one another by ties of kinship, so that political relations are co-terminous with kinship relations and the political structure and kinship organization are completely fused.[7]

In most African societies, then, kinship constitutes the primary basis for the individual's rights, duties, rules of residence, marriage, inheritance and succession. Malinowski was interested in the kinship system of the Trobrianders because it enabled him to understand the structural ties between individuals and the various institutional patterns in the society.

A clear distinction is made between types of kinship. Kinship may be said to be *cognatic* in structure. This means that the individual or Ego can trace descent through both parents. This is sometimes referred to as a bilateral system. The bilateral system means, theoretically, that both parents are equally important to Ego in social terms. Another type is the *agnatic* type which means that Ego's father's people are more important to him in social terms than his mother's people and thus he traces descent through the male line and all people in this line are his agnates.

PREGNANCY AND BIRTH OF A BABY

Pregnancy and birth are critical events in the life-cycle of every woman. Pregnancy of a newly-married woman brings joy to the families of both the man, and especially, the woman. It is a sign that the ancestral spirits on the man's side are sending a representative into the community, if the society is patrineally oriented. If it is matrilineally oriented, the contrary is true; the baby comes from the mother's ancestresses. It also establishes, and in a way, consummates the marriage; while it confirms the fecundity of the man. In most African societies, and this may be true in other societies, a woman's important ambition is to marry and that the marriage be fruitful. A woman who sees the signs of pregnancy after marriage becomes elated and announces the news with demur. For example, in the New Testament, we read of the unexpected pregnancy of Elizabeth. She broke forth in poetic adoration . . .

And after those days his wife Elizabeth was conceived, and
hid herself five months saying : 'Thus hath the Lord dealt with
me in the days wherein he looked on me, to take away my
reproach among men' (St Luke 1 : 24–5).

Pregnancy, therefore, has some carthartic effects on women. It reaffirms their femininity and gives expression to their maternal instinct. When pregnancy is firmly established, the early months of pregnancy are very important in the woman's life. The gestation period starts when the woman does not experience the monthly menses. Sometimes the symptoms may be expressed in the changing skin colour of the woman, or the heaviness of her breasts, which become very warm with darkened nipples. The other symptoms may be nausea and cravings for unusual food or loss of appetite or obesity and irritability. Some women tend to be very emotional and demand more attention from their husbands. The husbands may even be expected to encourage some degree of self-indulgence on the part of the pregnant woman. The pregnant woman's status in the community changes, and from the time she becomes pregnant to the time of delivery, she becomes a marginal member of the household and the community at large.

In most African societies, a pregnant woman is regarded as a *profane* object and at the same time sacred because of the fact that she is in both the spiritual and secular worlds. The terms I have used are analogous to the Durkheimian concept of religion. 'The definition of the religious phenomenon adopted by Durkheim is as follows: The essence of religion is to establish a division of the world into two kinds of phenomena, sacred, and profane.' (Raymond Aron, *Main Currents in Sociological Thought*, Penguin Books Ltd., Harmondsworth, Middx., England, 1967, p. 53.)

This bipartite division of the woman's existence into the sacred and profane means that certain religious beliefs are associated with pregnancy, and that certain ritual rules should be observed in interacting with her. She may in certain social situations be regarded as a source of danger, while in other situations, she may be regarded as a source of fortune. The pregnant woman is therefore not a normal person, but someone to be venerated, and at the same time to be feared. She too has to observe a series of taboos in her dealings with other members of the community.

The status of a pregnant woman and her treatment vary from one society to another. For example, Mbiti in his book *African Religions and Philosophy* observes that in some African societies pregnant women are regarded as 'impure' ritually. Because of her state of impurity she is not allowed to continue sexual intercourse with her husband. Mbiti goes on to say as follows:

'Another regulation concerns food: expectant mothers are forbidden to eat certain foods for fear that these foods would interfere with the health and safety of the mother or child, or would cause misfortune to either of them after birth. For example, among Akamba the expectant mother is forbidden to eat fat, beans, and meat of animals killed with poisoned arrows, during the last three months of pregnancy. In addition to other foods she eats a special kind of earth found on anthills or trees.' (John Mbiti, *African Religions and Philosophy*, Doubleday, Anchor Books, 1969, p. 44, para. 4.)

The pregnant woman is also expected to conduct herself with the utmost propriety in her relationship with other members of the family, and should maintain unflinching loyalty and fidelity to her husband. It is believed that strained relations between the pregnant woman and her husband may cause complications during the gestation period and may result in miscarriage, a sign of the displeasure of the husband's ancestors. Every potential tension or open conflict is therefore resolved instantaneously. The sun must not 'set' over the anger of the husband.

Any pregnant woman who bears a grudge against her husband or any member of the husband's family may experience difficulties. One of the first things a husband does as soon as his wife becomes pregnant is to put the wife in the care of a medicine man, or a midwife. Most older women in the community are virtually midwives. They build their knowledge on personal experiences and experiences gained by trial and error. The pregnant woman pays occasional visits to the medicine man or the midwife, or both to discuss ante-natal problems with them. The medicine man may pray for her, give her some herbs or roots for her food or enema, or she may take the medicine like a beverage. Sometimes, too, the pregnant woman may visit the lineage head of the man, who may pour libation and pray to the ancestral spirits by pouring of water or liquor on the ground while addressing the ancestral spirits.

Most pregnant women are very nervous and tense, because they are never sure about the normality of their developing babies during gestation period. In Western societies these anxieties and uncertainties are minimized by the improvement of gynaecological technology. Although there may be cases of still-born babies, the percentage in relation to developing countries are infinitesimal indeed. In most African societies these anxieties are minimized by complete dependence on nature and ancestral spirits. The future of the baby is determined by the ancestors, thus the whole idea of pregnancy and childbirth is given a deterministic orientation, and nothing could intervene to change the fate of the baby and the mother. This situation presents us with a philosophical problem. Nature on the whole is wasteful; and indiscriminate. Sometimes certain women who may be unfit to hold pregnancy may be helped by modern medicine to carry the baby through the period of gestation. Several results are possible. An ailing baby, with incurable, congenital disabilities may be born; or the side-effects of the medicine used may cause certain unintended harmful effects. All these may not have occurred if natural course had not been interferred with. The chances are that the baby would be miscarried by natural process. The Spencerian doctrine of the survival of the fittest, although outmoded by modern standards; it is consistent with African dogma of pregnancy and birth. At certain times, science does not predict rightly; for this reason, an unwanted baby who may have been got rid of during gestation by the natural process of miscarriage, is nurtured and brought into the world, becoming a burden on the parents.

The African believes that babies are gifts from the ancestors, and in fact, in some cases babies may possess characteristics and peculiarities of a dead member of the family. A clear distinction should be made between the doctrine of reincarnation and the endowment of certain characteristics which are similar to a dead ancestor's. Since the baby is already a member of the group, or the lineage in the spiritual world, it is taken for granted that it would be normal and healthy. A miscarriage presages unpreparedness on the part of the ancestors or the couple.

The difference between Western and African notion of pregnancy is the obvious certainty of the delivery of the baby, and, therefore, the preparation for the arrival of the baby. In most African societies, pregnancy is a very dicey thing, and it is viewed with appreciable reservations. For example, pregnant women do not make any preparations for the baby in terms of clothes. They do not search for names, because in the first place, the sex is not known, and any such expressed concern would be tantamount to 'counting ones chickens before they are hatched'.

The baby is not sure of until the day of delivery and a week after, when the baby assumes a given name, and the name of the day on which it is born.

Childbirth can take place anywhere in most societies. Sometimes babies are born on farms, or by the wayside. In some societies there are special places for childbirth, as for example the cases quoted by

Mbiti ... (ibid., p. 146, para. 1, seq.).

For example, the Udhuk custom is that when a women is about to deliver, she goes alone into the bush to give birth there. She might, however, ask a relative to go with her. The custom seems to have arisen from another custom by which a woman who gives birth to twins is killed together with the twins. By giving birth away from other people nobody would know if she gets twins, in which case she would kill one of the twins and return home with the other. This is an extreme custom and is not reported in other societies ...'

Childbirth is a critical event. When a pregnant woman sees signs of labour, a midwife is sent for at once. The midwife takes the woman into a room and helps her to deliver the baby. Men are not usually allowed to be present during the labouring period, unless there are complications, and it is believed that the cause of the difficulties is associated with something done by the wife against the husband. This may be deliberate or inadvertent, or covert or overt act. The husband then has to be there to perform certain rituals to facilitate birth.

It is believed that unborn babies are very intuitive to the point that they refuse to be born if there is any strained relations between a pregnant woman and her husband.

Sometimes there may be one midwife, but other times there may be more than one, and even a medicine man may be invited to help.

Birth is by natural method. Breathing exercise, holding of breath to build up enough pressure for pushing the baby down the enlarged uterus. Relaxation exercise in the pelvic area, making good use of muscular contraction, in a way not to choke or smother the baby. As soon as the baby is delivered, the midwife dips her fingers, maybe the index or two fingers in water, and moistens the lips of the baby. Thereupon if the baby is not still-born, it will yell. As soon as the baby cries, its sex is identified by the midwife, and she tells the mother immediately. The mother must know everything about the baby before the husband is told.

After the baby comes the placenta. Sometimes the placenta does not follow automatically, and the midwife has to help it out, by carefully pulling, while the woman continues to build up pressure to push it out. Some women have died during the ejection of the placenta. When the placenta is safely brought out, the umbilical cord is then severed. The placenta is taken away by a newly married maiden to bury in either the yard or outside of the house. Mbiti observes that in some African societies, the baby wears the placenta as a charm.

The placenta among other things is said to be a symbol of fertility and that it possesses a supernatural power that causes pregnancy. The placenta therefore has animatistic implications. Animatism is the belief in supernatural forces which inhabit ordinary objects or persons.

R. R. Marrett was the chief proponent of this idea. He maintained that there was the belief in supernatural powers without human personality among certain societies. The concept, he went on to say, was developed from another belief, the belief in *mana*. Mana is a word used by the Melanesians and the Polynesians for impersonal powers. Chiefs and ritual functionaries possess mana in varying degrees according to their ranks. An ordinary thing like stone if it is oddly shaped, and not like other stones, is thought to have mana.

'If a man plants such a stone in his garden, and if the yield
of yams increases he becomes convinced that there is mana in it.'

Such ways of thinking are not unique or peculiar only to the Melanesians and Polynesians. There is a clear distinction made between the lamp-post in the corner of a street, and an altar. The altar is regarded to be more 'sacred' than the lamp-post, among the Roman Catholics and Episcopalians.

Mana is sometimes thought to be both dangerous and beneficial. In some African societies the tools of a craftsman are said to be both beneficial and at the same time dangerous. For example, a carpenter may use his tools for building or making a table, but he may also use them for cursing enemies. Curiously enough the vagina is believed to be both beneficial and dangerous. Some women may use their vagina to curse a man that has mistreated them and bless a man who has been good to them. The placenta is therefore held in awe, and it is believed to have supernatural powers. This belief is supported by the fact that it is the bag in which the ancestors wrap up the baby, and it is the placenta that nurtures and keeps it for nine months.

The baby is still not a member of the community. Both the mother and the baby are removed from everyday contact with the outside world by the *rite of separation*, which places them in the realm of the sacred (meaning something set aside to be out of bounds to people). Only very close relatives are allowed to see the baby after it has been bathed, and the stains of blood have been removed, and it has been bundled up in swaddling clothes. On the eighth day they are brought out of seclusion into the community by the *rite of aggregation*. This will involve the mother wearing new clothes, usually white clothes, silver ear-rings and white beads. The baby is similarly clad, the father will give a name for the baby. This ceremony is the naming ceremony, which coincides with the 'outdooring', meaning the naming of the baby and introducing both the mother and the baby to the community. The mother and baby are showered with gifts from well-wishers and there is drinking and eating throughout the day. Where circumcision is practised, it is on the eighth day that circumcision is performed, for girls their ears are pierced. Most African societies observe patronymic rules in naming their children. Usually a name is selected from a living or dead member of the lineage, a friend, or improvised. Most names only have nostalgic, and sentimental symbolism, but in some African societies, they articulate specific messages. This is true among the Yorubas and the Ibos, sometimes the Ewe may have names with specific meanings. Among the Akans, the largest ethnic group in Ghana, individuals have two names, one which they automatically assume on the day they are born, and the family names which are conferred upon them by their fathers. This is why most Africans remember the day on which they are born and not the date, because they derive their first names from the day of their birth. The procedure of conferring names is very simple but it is essentially ubiquitous. There may be some fine variations, but the structure of the main ceremony follows a common pattern. During the period of separation, while the mother and the baby are cloistered, the father begins to search for a suitable name for the baby. He confers with an older member of his family or his parents to give him some suggestions of names. Sometimes a lineage head who knows the history of the lineage and is conversant with the genealogy, is consulted.

The adoption of names is dictated by biographical and social considerations. In adopting a name for one's child great premium is placed on the historical associations of the name to be adopted. If the name reminds the family of a miscreant, then the intention is dropped, and another name is considered. Usually fathers will confer on their first born, names of either their mothers or their fathers, that is the names of the grandparents of the new-born baby. In some cases the names of their brothers or sisters are adopted. In such circumstances, it is not necessary to consult anyone in the family.

Names are therefore the mnemonics of the aspirations and the future dreams one has for his/her child. Names of persons with doubtful reputation and questionable biography are never adopted, because it is believed that bearers of names assume certain idiosyncrasies, and peculiarities of peoples whose names they assume. When the names conferred on the baby are those of an important person in the family then the baby is accorded similar deference and social recognition. For example, once the baby assumes the name, it is called 'father' or 'mother' as the case may be by all the people who address the original bearer of the name as such, and if 'grandfather' or 'grandmother' then all the people who have previously addressed the original bearer as such now have to address the new-born baby similarly, including children of his own generation. The mechanics of the actual conferring of names vary from culture to culture. For example, among the Akans the father and a few relatives of the wife and some friends, including his relatives, meet at the house of the father of the baby or the family house. The oldest member of the family will then be charged with the responsibility of naming the child. The name will be announced, and the master of the ceremony for the occasion will pour libation, invoking the ancestral spirits and their blessings on the new member of the family.

REFERENCES

1 Carol Ember and Melvin Ember, *Cultural Anthropology*, 2nd edition, Prentice-Hall Inc. Englewood-Cliff, N.J., 1977, p. 40, para. 6.

2 David Schulz, *The Changing Family: Its Function and Future*, 2nd edition, Prentice-Hall Inc., N.J., 1976, p. 19.

3 T. B. Bottomore, *Sociology*, London: Allen and Unwin, 1962, p. 62.

4 *Notes and Queries in Anthropology*, p. 72.

5 Radcliffe-Brown and Forde (eds.), 1950, p. 5.

6 M. Fortes, *The Dynamics of Clanship among the Tallensi*, London: Oxford University Press, 1945; and *The Web of Kinship Among the Tallensi*, London: Oxford University Press, 1949.

7 M. Fortes and E. E. Evans-Pritchard, Introduction to *African Political Systems*, London: International African Institute, Oxford University Press, 1940, p. 6.

IV

Household and Lineage

RULES OF residence may tend to encourage the congregation of a number of people who are related to one another either by affinity or birth. Apart from the heads of single families, there may be other kinship ties woven into the group thus forming 'a web of kinship'. This group may now be bigger than a family and may be described as a *household*. According to Professor I. Schapera:

> The smallest well-defined unit in the social system of the Tswana is the household, a group of people occupying the same enclosure of huts. It consists basically of a man with his wife or wives and their unmarried children, but often also includes one or more married sons, brothers or even daughters with their respective spouses and children. It may contain up to fifteen people, occasionally more, but the general average is from five to seven.[1]

The household in most societies is a corporate group owning common property, and it constitutes the unit of production and consumption. Since some of the members are related to each other by reason of the fact of having descended from either a common father or mother at a certain genealogical level, this relationship becomes rather far removed from the original source, and any meaningful description of this type of relationship can only be by reference to the ancestor of the group either dead or alive. Anthropologists use a term which describes this relationship succinctly— *a lineage group*.

A lineage group is the result of social accretion caused by common habitation of kinsmen. Every member of a lineage claims to be related to every member of that group by direct descent or descent from a common ancestor (patrilineal) or ancestress (matrilineal).

28

Professor Raymond Firth describes lineage as

a unilineal descent group, all members of which trace their genealogical relationship back to a founding ancestor. If the lineage is patrilineal (or agnatic), the members consist of men, their children and their sisters, and trace their descent through males and normally to an original ancestor. If the system is matrilineal, the members consist of women, their children, and their brothers, tracing descent through females, and normally to an original ancestress. Such groups are exogamous. A series of households may form larger social groups which are known as CLANS. A clan is a unilineal descent group of major order in a society acting as a unit in a system of similar groups. The separate clans in a system are usually named and are often distinguished symbolically by associations of a totemic kind with natural species. Clans usually have some corporate functions of a political or ritual order, and may play a very important part in community life. Clan members normally regard one another as kinsfolk, though they may not be able to trace their relationship genealogically. Frequently they express this relationship in rules of exogamy whereby a member must marry outside his clan.[2]

Both the lineage and the clan are exogamous groups, they are corporate, and have many things in common. The difference between lineage and clan is that members of a lineage can trace the founding ancestor, whether dead or alive, and may be placed on a genealogical chart, while members of a clan cannot trace the founding ancestor, because he is putative and may be represented by animals or natural objects. Among the Aborigines in Australia, kangaroos may be totemic symbols or ancestors.

Both lineages and clans can only be meaningful by reference to their social functions in relation to certain social practices such as exogamy and incest prohibition. (Rules of incest prohibition mean that certain categories of relationship impose restrictions on sexual congress.) But the importance of the lineage and its use are evident in the political context and the rules which they prescribe for descent systems.[3]

Since I shall be discussing the political aspect of the lineage in another context, I want to mention, in passing, certain important points about the lineage. The lineage, as I have already indicated, is larger than the nuclear family and it embraces several generations of kin-groups. It may be very wide with a span of six to nine generations. Sometimes it may be even bigger making the founder so distant that structural ties begin to weaken. There is therefore a deliberate segmentation of lineage; that is, internal splitting of lineages. Fortes in his studies of the Tale society distinguished five segments of varying depth and span. Evans-Pritchard found four among the Nuer. The *minimal lineage* categorized by Fortes is similar to the nuclear family, but slightly larger since it is two or three generations in depth and provides the individual member of this lineage with the right of cultivation of lands belonging to the *nuclear lineage* of four to six generations depth. Legal affairs (such as marriage or compensation for seduction) and ritual matters (such as funerals) are managed by the *inner lineage* of five to seven generations depth. The *medial lineage* includes

'two or more inner lineages ...
Its founding ancestor may be placed from six to eight or nine generations back.... A significant index of the medial lineage is that it marks the limits within which a man is prohibited from marrying a patrilineal kinswoman of his mother.'[4]

The *maximal lineage* which is the largest group is charged with the responsibility of local political organization.

Segmentation of lineage groupings is also important among the Nuer. It facilitates individuals' self-identification in the larger group of the society. Evans-Pritchard observes that,

On the structural plane, there is always contradiction in the definition of a political group, for a man is a member of it in virtue of his non-membership of other groups of the same type.[5]

and 'social cohesion increases as the size of the community narrows'.[6]

REFERENCES

1 I. Schapera, 'Kinship on Marriage among the Tswana,' in Radcliffe-Brown and Forde (eds.), p. 141.

2 Firth, *Human Types*, London: Nelson, 1956, p. 112.

3 See M. Fortes, *Web of Kinship* (1949), for a functional analysis of the lineage structure among the Tallensi in Ghana.

4 M. Fortes, 1949, p. 10.

5 E. E. Evans-Pritchard, *The Nuer*, Oxford: The Clarendon Press, 1940.

6 Evans-Pritchard, 1940, p. 162.

V

Descent Systems in Africa: Inheritance and Succession

In Africa, people are grouped according to certain principles, which are referred to in the literature as descent principles. By these principles it is possible to classify a group of people as kinsmen or relatives. They describe themselves by terms which are used only for near relatives, e.g., 'brother' for almost all the members of the group in the same generation. Similarly, the terms father or mother are used for people of one's father's or mother's generation. A man may therefore call 'brother' not only a father's son, but his father's sons and other first or second cousins of his own generation. This is what is called in anthropology the *classificatory system of kinship terminology*. A group of people who regard themselves as related in this way do so because they believe that they have descended from the same ancestor or ancestress. If descent is traced through the male line to a common ancestor, then the group so formed is called a patrilineal group or society. If, on the other hand, descent is traced through the female line, then the group or society is matrilineal.

The social implications of dividing societies into these opposing categories are that it is believed that in Africa a distinction is made between sociological paternity (*pater*) and biological paternity (*genitor*). Among the Ashanti of Ghana, it is said that one's mother's people are more important in many ways than one's father's people. It means that the individual in a matrilineal society derives all his jural rights from his mother's people. The idea which is attached to this belief in Ashanti is that an individual is compounded of two parts, blood and spirit. Dr. K. A. Busia spells this out:

Ashanti chiefship is based on the lineage system. The theory of procreation held is that a human being is compounded of two principles—the blood (mogya) which he inherits from the mother and the other, spirit (ntoro), which is derived from the father.[1]

Recent anthropological writings, however, have come out with new ideas about this concept of unilineal descent, and a flood of light has been shed on certain weak aspects of the dogma of unilineality. Fortes anticipated this new idea in his studies of both the Ashanti and the Tallensi. He found that although these two societies could be described as unilineal, they had certain aspects which gave them a different character which should be taken into account. Among the Ashanti, a matrilineal society, he found that the father had a special ritual link with his children (ntoro) with corresponding obligations on either side. For example, the father has to name his children, marry for his sons and provide them with a gun, if illiterate. In modern times, most fathers give their children education. The children, too, have to perform certain services such as mortuary rites which include the provision of their deceased father's coffin. Among the Tallensi, a patrilineal society, the mother's people start their nephews with a few chickens for their poultry farms. Fortes, therefore, coined a new term, *complementary filiation* to emphasize the fact that societies cannot be arranged neatly in opposing categories—matrilineal and patrilineal. New terms used are patrifiliation for societies with patrilineal emphasis and matrifiliation for societies with a matrilineal accent.[2] In all societies, however, the relationship between a child and his parents contains a high degree of emotional warmth. Whatever custom may prescribe, in real life people may behave differently.

From the preceding chapters, we have seen that people are admitted into a group by birth or descent. The process by which a man acquires membership of a kin group is termed *descent*. The process by which he acquires rank and privileges is termed *succession*, and the way in which property is transmitted to another after the death of the original owner is termed *inheritance*. The processes by which a person acquires either membership of a kinship group, inherits property or succeeds to an office may take place through one parent or both. When this is only permitted through one parent, it is called *unilateral*. When it is permitted through two parents, it is referred to as *bilateral*.

33

In most African societies, people inherit property and succeed to ranks through one line—either matrilineally or patrilineally. Among the Ashanti, children may only succeed to ranks in their mother's lineage, but certain titles, especially royal titles, may be succeeded to in the paternal line. This is different from patrilineal succession. For example in Aburi, among the Akwapim, an Akan tribe which is a matrilineal, sons of chiefs are eligible to an office known as Ahemmahene. This patrilineal institution is important in the political system, because occupants of this office are ex-officio members of the king maker's committee or the conclave which is charged with responsibility of selecting a new chief.

Items of inheritance in most African societies were simple indeed. In a subsistence economy, accumulation of wealth was non-existent. People only inherited farm produce, livestock, and some personal effects. Among the Yako of Eastern Nigeria, the principles which govern descent allow for the recognition of inheritance operating in both lines. The societies are organized in patrilineages and matrilineages with accompanying jural rights and obligations. The rights to dwelling sites, land for purposes of farming, and the more important forest resources are obtained through one's patrilineal links. On the other hand, currency, whether it be in brass rods or modern coinage, and all livestock should by custom pass to matrilineal relatives who also receive the greater share of the implements, weapons, household goods and food.[3] Here a distinction is made between transmittable goods and immovable property. Immovable items of inheritance go from father to children and transmittable goods go from mother to children.

There are bases for tension in all systems of inheritance, and these inherent tensions have been aggravated by economic changes. Where polygamous marriage exists, there will always be more beneficiaries competing for a limited property. Here inheritance becomes a litigious affair. Land tenure also contributes largely to the apparent difficulties of inheritance. Titles to land ownership are not transferable. Land is owned by groups of people and administered by trustees of elders and chiefs of the communities, whether tribes, clans or lineages. Members are allowed the usufructuary rights over land—they cannot treat these rights as exclusive personal rights which could be inherited by one's successor. There is, however, strife in the inheritance practice owing to the economic

34

exploitation of land. Plantation farming has changed the pattern of land tenure because a piece of land may remain in the possession of a family for as long as it is being used, and may even be treated as a right under the law of tort, which permits transmission of the land with the crops to successors in the family. The religious aspect of land has given way to the economic value of land. It is no more the home of the ancestral spirits, but capital for the living.

REFERENCES

1 K. A. Busia, *The Position of the Chief in the Modern Political System of Ashanti*, London: Oxford University Press, 1951, p. 1.

2 E. R. Leach, *Re-thinking Anthropology*, London: University of London Athlone Press, 1961, p. 58. See also M. Fortes, 'Submerged Descent line in Ashanti' in Studies in Kinship and marriage: Dedicated to Brenda Z. Seligman on her 80th birthday, I. Schapera (ed.), *Royal Anthropological Inst. Occ. Pap.* No. 16, London: 1963, pp. vi, 114.

3 C. Daryll Forde, 'Double Descent among the Yako', in Radcliffe-Brown and Forde (eds.), p. 311.

VI

Dynamics of Kinship Terminology
in Small-scale Societies

KINSHIP REFERS to a particular category of relationships which exist between two individuals, or a group of individuals. These are relationships which may have their roots in common genealogy, or may be effected through marriage or adoption. For example, a grandchild is descended from a grandparent and both may have descended from a common ancestor or ancestress. Sometimes the term consanguinity is used for describing these categories of kinship ties. But the term consanguinity is loaded with definite connotations, which do not fit the anthropological usage of the concept of kinship. Consanguinity stresses the biological aspect of kinship while what anthropologists are interested in is the sociological aspect of kinship. When anthropologists talk about descent they mean the pater's ties with Ego and not the genitor's—even if both are the same persons. (Pater in this case means the social father, and genitor means the biological father.) Kinship generally refers to specific social arrangements[1] and the ordering of social interactions in society. The study of kinship is important because it is the mnemonics of certain fundamental social arrangements and norms in most societies. Radcliffe-Brown who has done pioneering work in the field of kinship studies observed as follows:

> One common feature of kinship system is the recognition
> of certain categories or kinds into which the various relatives of
> a single person can be grouped. The actual social relation
> between a person and his relative, as defined by rights and
> duties and modes of behaviour is then to a greater or less
> extent fixed by the category to which the relative belongs.
> The nomenclature of kinship is commonly used as a means of
> establishing and recognising these categories. A single term

may be used to refer to a category of relatives and different categories will be distinguished by different terms.[2]

A similar view is held by Radcliffe-Brown.

Kinship therefore results from the recognition of a social relationship between parents and children, which is not the same thing as physical relation, and may not coincide with it.[3]

The relationships which exist between individuals are expressed in definite terms, thus conceptualizing the norms and the code of behaviour or the type of interactions, either open-ended or restricted, that should operate between these various categories of individuals who are thus connected. The history of kinship goes back to the eighteenth century when Lafitau published the result of his research among American Indians.

Among the Iroquois and Hurons all the children of a cabin regard all their mother's brothers as their uncles, and for the same reason they give the name of father to all their father's brothers, and aunts to all their father's sisters. All the children on the side of the mother and her sisters, and of the father and his brothers, regard each other mutually as brothers and sisters, but as regards the children of their uncles and aunts, that is, of their mother's brothers and father's sisters, they only treat them on the footing of cousins.[4]

This discovery triggered off more interest in the study of kinship systems and their functions in the society. Lewis Morgan looked more closely at the same society and in 1871 he produced his 'Systems of Consanguinity and Affinity', thus proving the validity of Lafitau's thesis, but this time coining a term for this social arrangement ... 'classificatory terminology'.

According to Morgan the classification of a cluster of kinship ties, which means using the terms intended for lineal relatives for certain collateral relatives facilitates the ordering of complex kinship ties in societies where these ties are important.

The distinguishing feature of a classificatory system of terminology in Morgan's usage is that terms which apply to lineal relatives are also applied to certain collateral relatives. Thus a father's brother is father and mother's sister is 'mother', while as in the type described by Lafitau, there are separate terms for mother's brother, and father's brother and mother's sisters are called 'brother' and 'sister' and there are separate terms for the children of mother's brothers and father's sisters.... A man classifies the children of his brothers with his own children, but uses a separate term for the children of his sister. Inversely a woman classifies with her own children the children of her sisters but not those of her brothers. Classificatory terminologies of the kind are found in a great many African peoples.[5]

Before I go on to examine the social implications of these classificatory systems I would just mention in parenthesis another kinship terminology known as 'descriptive terminology'.

Descriptive terminology is useful when specific and narrow-span relationships are to be identified: for example when first or second order relatives are to be specified. In this case compounds of specific terms are applied. This takes the form of 'mother's brother' for one's maternal uncle and father's brother for one's paternal uncle and so on. This system is more specific than the English term Uncle or Aunt if the descriptive terminology is preferred to the classificatory system; it is useful only for analytical purposes.

This system is rarely used except when specification of relationships is necessary for definite social purposes. The classificatory system of kinship terminology is however important in societies in which kinship determines one's place in them, and prescribes his code of behaviour vis-à-vis other people in the society. Most small-scale societies employ the classificatory systems, as observed by Raymond Firth.

The classificatory system of relationship has been often enough described, so that its general features are familiar. What has not so often been realized, though, is the function of such a system as a stabilizing mechanism in a society. It forms a most useful mode of grouping people: it establishes their relation to one another. Looked at from this point of view, the old contrast with systems of the descriptive type is meaningless;

within a classificatory system it is perfectly possible to
describe individuals by modification or qualification of terms,
or by additional terms for special relatives—all of which
phenomena are frequent in primitive kinship.[6]

Classificatory terminology serves as an indicator to people who are
immersed in a 'web of kinship' for appropriate social behaviour;
this fact is the core of Leach's observation in his recent book on
Levi Strauss.

Most kinship facts present themselves to the field
anthropologist in two ways. In the first place as I have said
his informants use a kinship terminology, words like father,
mother, uncle, cousin etc. to sort out the people in their
vicinity into significant groups, but secondly it emerges that
there are various sets of behaviours and attitudes which are
considered especially appropriate or inappropriate as between
any two individuals deemed to be related in a particular way.
—e.g. It may be said that a man should never speak in the
presence of his mother-in-law or that it would be a good thing
if he were to marry a girl who falls into the same kin term
class as his mother's brother's daughter.
If we are trying to understand the day-to-day behaviour of
people living in close face-to-face relationship, facts such as
these are clearly of great significance and a good deal of the
field anthropologist's research time is taken up with discovering
just how these two frames of reference—the system of verbal
categories and the system of behavioural attitudes—are
inter-connected....[7]

Most anthropologists have given kinship terminology due attention
in their studies of primitive peoples. For example, Fortes, in his
classical studies among the Tallensi of northern Ghana, appeared
to imply that kinship was the only means by which any meaningful
studies could be undertaken among these people. He observed as
follows:

The Tallensi apply the concepts of kinship to describe and
define domestic relations and person-to-person ties that are

derived from them. They use the same concepts in dealing with lineage relation. In the social structure as a whole, kinship is the fundamental binding element. It furnishes the primary axioms of all categories of interpersonal and intergroup relations.[8]

Kinship is not only pervasive, but it is the idiom through which the Tale social system is expressed in any meaningful sense. The terms which are used to express the values of kinship enjoin the individual men who are described in these social contexts to behave within the customarily prescribed meaning of the terms used. The syntax in the term is not merely rhetorical but morally obligatory. When people who are described as classificatory relatives behave as enemies or strangers social conscience is as outraged as if the attitude existed between lineal relatives. Sometimes classificatory terminology is used for describing tribal groups; members of the same tribal groups may therefore treat each other as brothers or lineal relatives expecting appropriate treatment from each other. Kinship terminology, particularly the classificatory type, is inextricably linked with inheritance and succession. This is in cases where inheritance and succession are not lineal, that is, they are neither by primogeniture nor direct to first generation. Succession to any office is generational.

A group of collaterals of the same generation may all be eligible to a particular office within the group, and therefore the right to inherit any property associated with this office is not restricted to any one particular person. Kinship therefore confers on individuals common ascriptive status and privileges, especially to members of a royal family. Sometimes a particular office may be of a unique character so that only a core within a social group has any right to this office. I call this type of succession arrangement 'extended-primogeniture' because succession runs lineally through that line, within a prescribed perimeter. Dr Audrey I. Richards observed that among the societies which do not possess any institution with centralized political authority, certain types of people are collectively treated with deference by others and they constitute what anthropologists call 'dominant clans'.

In most of the traditional African societies known to us,

authority tends to be associated with special lines of descent. In the case of segmented societies, which acknowledge neither a single chief nor a series of chiefs, these descent lines are usually called dominant clans, aristocratic noble lineages, or land-owner lines. These privileged descent groups form part of a social structure in which commoners as well as nobles base their status on descent, and kinship usually determines their pattern of settlement and economic life.[9]

My own experiences among the Akwapim, among whom I did my field work, reinforce the above thesis. Kinship is the matrix of social interactions and the social field is marked and punctuated by kinship ramifications. In the field of social stratification, kinship confers on certain individuals certain rights over others, thus placing some people in asymmetrical social juxtaposition vis-à-vis others in the societies. Even in political rights, where they are not legitimized by charismatic considerations, kinship credentials confer certain rights over others, and individuals are ascribed certain rights within their group. Audrey Richards is very lucid on the point of the transfer of political authority, or the mechanism by which political élites are recruited in most traditional African societies. She based her exposition on kinship paradigm as the criterion of political recruitment, as this affects the higher reaches of political ranking.

By Political Rights I shall refer to the claims maintained by a person or a group to the exercise of power or privilege, or position of social precedence—claims which are considered legitimate in the community concerned in the sense that they are accepted as rightful dues. I include for this purpose the claims of an office-holder such as a King, a territorial chief, a clan or a lineage head or a religious functionary, or, in the case of an acephalous society, the rights of some corporate group such as a major lineage, which considers itself entitled to economic, ritual or other privilege. Such claims are invariably based on precedent. This is in fact what we mean by traditional political right. Some version of historical events gives the privileged the right to enjoy political authority—some myth however fantastic, some legend of migration, conquest or the occupation of new territory, however ill-attested, some line of descent however truncated—versions of the past which social anthropologists now group together loosely under the heading 'historical charters' following and slightly extending Malinowski's (1926) original use of the term.[10]

The legitimization of political authority at every level, according to Audrey Richards, is based on what she calls 'historical charters', and in the final analysis, descent and therefore kinship predominates among the characteristics of the various political rights. My own field experience among the Akwapim reinforces Audrey Richards's point.

The people who are called the Akwapim inhabit part of the Akwapim-Ewe range of hills. The area occupies the hill country north of Accra, the capital of Ghana; sixteen of its towns lie in line along the crest of the main ridge. Historically the Akwapim were mainly Guans, but were assisted in a war against a tribe known as Akwamus by the Akyems, another tribe from the eastern side of Ghana. After the conquest, the Akyem mercenaries decided to settle on the ridge and they set out to reorganize the political and social structure of Akwapim. The Akyems are culturally Akans; and as a result of this historical event the Akans who are immigrants to Akwapim now constitute the dominant groups. The Akans in Akwapim are organized in structures. The dominant lineage which forms the paramountcy, may be described by the various terms viz. proximate, contiguous, and dispersed. The various segments of the paramountcy are so described because they are integral part of the paramountcy. The core of the paramountcy is traditionally called 'Nkonguasonfo' or 'Koman' (* See Appendix on p. 105). Nkonguason literally means seven stools. When the suffix 'fo' is attached to it, it means occupants of seven stools. This term is a logical derivation from the military origins of the immigration of the Akyems. The forebears of all the Akans in the Akwapim State gave military aid to the aboriginal Akwapim people in the early eighteenth century, and in recognition of their military prowess, and victories over the Akwamus, they were asked to remain in Akwapim and protect the people.[11]

The political pre-eminence of the Akans particularly the Akyems over the Guans, the aborigines, is based on 'historical charters' of military intervention and military aid. This point of ascriptive political right is common among most African societies, and its pervasiveness is linked with an accepted jural equality among members of a particular clan or tribe who claim the right to such political authority. Professor M. Fortes, in his lucid and most illuminating synopsis of his new book on kinship, observes that kinship ties which form the basis of one's status may be relevant in both sides of an individual's parenthood, and this is a departure from the orthodox belief in unilinealty which dominated anthropology when the problems confronting the subject were mainly those of structural analysis. Nowadays, thanks to Fortes and his colleagues, African societies are not said to exhibit the type of bizarre features, portraying African societies a little less human than the western type which, according to the anthropological evolutionists, were at the top of the evolutionary ladder of civilization.

Professor Fortes has this to say on this matter:

Characteristically, owing to the jural equality of men and women in cognatic systems, 'kindred' connexions by filiation on either side of parenthood confer equal or parallel credential of eligibility of citizenship in the political community and hence succession.[12]

By rules of exogamy and preferential marriages, both working in complementary opposition, we find that most of the Akans in Akwapim wield some degree of political power which is ascribed to them either by reason of the father's lineage or mother's lineage. Here the Akans of the Akwapim State have common cultural features with those of the Tiv in their social structures. The dominant group of Akyem descendants in Akwapim claims descent from Akim Abuakwa. The Tiv according to Bohannan is a Tiv, because he descended from Tiv, the eponymous founder of the State. The Tiv do not present that difficulty so common to Africa; identifying the tribe. A Tiv is a Tiv and can prove it. This proof consists in a genealogy through which every Tiv can trace his descent from Tiv himself.

A similar idea underlies the use of genealogies in most Akan Societies, i.e. to trace descent from a clan founder, putative or real.

Kinship studies continue to attract interest because of their significance for many African societies in organizing their lives.

But there are some negative aspects of this subject which have been neglected. For example when classificatory kinship terminology is used for describing tribal groups, this then lifts the meaning on to a different level. It may develop into political rivalries, or alignments. In most modern African states, tribal nepotism seems to derive from the classificatory kinship system and it constitutes a cause of conflict and tension within the body-politic. The cause of the Nigerian civil war is well-known to us all—the Ibos of the south against the Western Nigerians. In Ghana too ethnic alignment based on common cultural and geographical identity manifested itself in its ugliest form in the Ashanti region. The polarization of interests expressed in the formation of a movement known as the National Liberation Movement (N.L.M.) to seize political power from the southerners developed into tribal warfare with concomitant disruption of efforts to attain independence at the time when this objective was in sight. The unrest and political rivalries which gripped the region were set out in a Report of a Commission of Inquiry which sat under Mr. Justice Jackson:

These few days, between the November 2 and 7, 1951, were certainly ones in which any man or woman who happened to be a member of the Convention People's Party was a hare and in which any supporter of the Wenchihene was a hound.[13]

The Ashantis at this time quarrelled among themselves on ideological grounds; this time it was fission within the tribal group, because of the C.P.P. epitomized a non-Ashanti nationalism and supporters were regarded as *persona non grata*, and branded as disloyal to the Ashanti cause.

The last General Elections were unfortunately plunged into tribal squabbles.

The performance of the seemingly Ewe-dominated N.L.C. Administration left a rather bad taste in many people's mouths because it was claimed that the leaders were practising nepotism, a largely baseless allegation. Gbedemah projected Ewe-tribal nationalism, and Busia Akan nationalism at the expense of national unity. Unfortunately this trend continues.[14]

In most modern states in Africa conventional social usages and traditional systems impinge on the newly structured policies. The latter have foreign bases, and their legitimization is becoming so dubious, that tensions and conflicts arise between the traditional political and legal-rational authority.

REFERENCES

1 E. Leach, *Levi-Strauss*, Fontana Modern Masters, Collins, 1970, p. 96. 'When anthropologists talk about kinship they are concerned with social behaviours and not biological facts and the two sets of data are often so widely discrepant that it is often convenient to discuss kinship without any reference to biology'.

2 Radcliffe-Brown, 1952, p. 62 *et seq.*

3 Radcliffe-Brown and Forde (eds.), 1950, p. 4.

4 Radcliffe-Brown and Forde (eds.), 1950, p. 8.

5 Radcliffe-Brown and Forde (eds.), 1950.

6 R. Firth, *We The Tikopia*, Beacon Press, 1963, p. 222, para. 1.

7 Leach, 1970, p. 97.

8 Fortes, 1949, p. 13.

9 A. I. Richards, 'Chiefs and their Royal Relatives', Presidential Address, *Journ. Roy. Anthropological Inst.*, Vol. 91, 1961, p. 1 *et seq.*

10 A. I. Richards, 'Social Mechanism for the transfer of political rights in some African Tribes', Presidential Address, *Journ. Roy. Anthropological Inst.*, Vol. 90, part 2, 1960, para. 2, et seq.

11 E. O. Ayisi, 1965, 'The Internal structure of the Paramountcy' in *The basis of political authority of the Akwapim Tribes*, unpublished doctoral thesis (London University), p. 214.

12 M. Fortes, Synopsis of: 'Kinship and the Social Order': *The Legacy of L. H. Morgan* (unpublished).

13 Commission of enquiry into Wenchi Affairs, Mr. Justice Jackson, p. 18, para. 117.

14 E. O. Ayisi, 'Ghana and the Return to Parliamentary Government', *Political Quarterly*, Vol. 41, No. 40b, 1970.

VII

Mechanics of Social Adjustment

IN MOST African societies, the changes which occur in the lives of individuals are marked by special initiation ceremonies. These ceremonies vary from one society to another and they are more dramatic in some societies than others. They may take the form of rites which involve the mutilation of certain parts of the individual. The term rite-de-passage is used collectively for all forms of ritual in a conceptual framework meaningful in all social situations. It is associated with the name of Van Gennep, an associate of Emile Durkheim. Van Gennep argued that in most simple societies changes which occurred in human experiences were ritualized—changes in the social status of individuals and all social activities which involved the full participation of the whole community. We shall discuss in this chapter the changes in the social status of individuals.

The custom of ritualizing the changes which occur in the life of the individual starts from cradle to the grave (birth, adolescence, marriage, election to an office, and mortuary rites). The people of Israel, for example, performed special rites for all first-born males. The Law of Moses enjoined the people to perform a special offering to the Lord for 'every male that openeth the womb shall be called holy to the Lord, and offer a sacrifice according to that which is said in the law of the land. A pair of turtle doves and two young pigeons'. (St Luke 2: 22-23).

In East Africa the ritual of transition takes the form of initiation of both boys and girls.[1] Boys are initiated in peer groups. Thus after initiation, age-sets are formed and have enduring political and social significance. The initiation ceremony takes the form of the trimming of the genital organs of both sexes. The ceremony is elaborate and complicated. The circumcision of girls, or clitoridectomy is common only in East Africa and some parts of Northern Ghana and Northern Nigeria. Once a girl has gone through this ceremony her status changes to something higher. In some cultures

46

initiation consists of a simple single rite at puberty. It may also be multiple when every stage of the individual's growth is marked by a series of rites covering the life cycle from cradle to the grave.

Initiation ceremonies are accompanied, in some cases, by the subjection of the novice to excruciating bodily and mental pain. This infliction of torture is regarded as a test of fortitude and a conditioning to pain and discomfort which the new life in which the individual finds himself will bring in its train. Sometimes the pain so inflicted is transitory, but at other times the pain leaves permanent marks on the victim:

> Sometimes the ordeals are transitory, consisting of such trials as whipping, being choked by smoke or bathing in ice-cold water. More frequently they are such as to leave permanent marks; thus among the Nuer boys are initiated by the cutting of the flesh of the forehead to the bone, thus making six horizontal scars extending from ear to ear which are plainly visible for the remainder of the individual's lifetime.[2]

Boys are circumcised and admitted into a new status, such as warriors in East Africa, and are then allowed to participate in adult life. Among the Akans, boys' initiation is not important and is not practised. The initiation of girls is more dramatic, but no physical mutilation is involved. When a girl starts to see her menses, she tells her mother about it and the mother will break the news to the girl's father. The girl is now ready for the initiation ceremony, but usually a girl may see more than three menstrual periods before the ceremony is performed. The ceremony involves some expense so that the parents need some time to get ready for it. When the parents are ready, they will wait until the next menstrual period and then the mother will inform her relatives and friends that the girl is of age and that on such and such a day she will be initiated. The evening of the day is a great evening of festivity. The girl's mother, her relatives and friends gather near the house of the girl, usually outside the house, and sing ritual songs rejoicing that the girl has now become a woman. The girl's friends participate in the singing and in the evening, the girl is carried by close kin to the riverside for the ritual bath by her sister with friends looking on. After the ritual bath, the girl becomes a woman and wears two pieces of cloth—one round her loins and the other piece over her shoulders, and a head tie. The ceremony goes on for six days and every evening young men and women gather at the spot for all sorts of 'love-games'. On the sixth day the girl dresses according to her new status and goes round thanking well-wishers and people who have given her presents. At this time if any young man is interested in this girl, he comes forward and gives her presents. The Fantis, also a group of the Akans, parade the girl dressed up in rich beads (*wo* hye hye no) and jewellery with her lovely breasts exposed on the sixth day when she goes round to thank people. The Gas[3] do the same thing—the girl is exposed from the waist up and dressed with rich beads. (Otofo).

The initiation also has political and educational implications. In its educational aspect it helps the individual to learn about the tradition of the society and to understand his duties and privileges. The sociological function of this ceremony is said to transmit cultural equipment, knowledge, skills, values and social sentiments to the individual members of the community. Its psychological function is to mould the growing individual in accordance with the rules of the community and to direct the development of the personality of such an individual along the lines which the community considers to be good.

EDUCATION IN PRIMITIVE SOCIETY THROUGH INITIATION

Education in primitive society is different from that in Western society in content and methodology. Methods of education of primitive peoples are pragmatic, entailing the practising of social activities. The learner participates in the real social situation. For example, a small boy watches his father and other male relatives making a canoe and will help them in running little errands, and in this way he will learn certain aspects of canoe-making. Piddington describes the system thus:

> At length by a series of such acts of imitation of, or
> participation in, the technical activity concerned, he
> finally becomes a skilled craftsman.[4]

Much of what the child learns is acquired in real life as opposed to artificial training situations. It is like the 'kindergarten' system

48

except that what happens in this context is necessary to the life of the community at the time it is happening.

The content of primitive education is simple, but very comprehensive. The system in its actual operation varies from complex communities with regard to method, personnel, content, and the motives and attitudes underlying the educational process.[5]

Methods: Training is a by-product of social activity.

Personnel: The personal agents in the primitive educational process consist primarily of kinsfolk and neighbours and older playmates.

Content: Transmission of knowledge and skills on the one hand and sentiments and values on the other hand.

Motives and attitudes underlying the educational process: The basic motivation is to train the children and also to help members of the communities to pass from one phase of life to the other with less frustration and difficulty.

The political implications in the initiation ceremony are more far-reaching than in the other already adumbrated. In the case of the initiation of chiefs or people holding ritual offices, the initiation follows a strict procedure of various stages of ritual observance.

THE MECHANICS OF INSTALLATION OF CHIEFS AND RITUAL FUNCTIONARIES AS PART OF INITIATION CEREMONY

The ritual procedures for appointing new chiefs and ritual officers are essentially uniform in all small-scale societies. I shall take the system in Akwapim, Ghana, to illustrate the mechanics of the installation ceremony, because Akwapim offers a good example of both a matrilineally and patrilineally oriented society. The people are made up of a congery of two main distinct ethnic groups who inhabit a common geographical area federated in a political organization with a military posture. Some of the tribes speak Guan and Kyerepong and trace descent to common ancestors, and some speak Akan or Twi and trace descent to common ancestresses. The Akan, mainly from Akyem,[6] the largest group of the Akwapim, are said to have come to the Ridge in 1722 to assist the Guans in a battle against the Akwamus led by their King Ansah Sasraku.[7]

There has been a cultural fusion in many ways, on the Akan model, yet in other matters such as esoteric idiosyncrasies, distinct ethnic groups have remained independent, keeping their peculiar beliefs intact. The Akans, for example, trace descent to common ancestresses while the Guans trace descent to common ancestors. The Guans observe the Ohum Festival, the time of remembrance of the dead, while the Akans observe only the Odwira, which serves both as a remembrance ceremony and a rite of purification of the stools and communion with the ancestral spirits. (See Chapter XI).

Each town of the 17 settlements is made up of lineage and clan segments and some of the lineages and clans claim social pre-eminence by reason of some truncated historical origins. These are royal lineages or clans and they provide chiefs and ritual officers. When a stool falls vacant by reason of the death or destoolment of the incumbent, the leader of the 'king-makers', the Kurontihene,[8] approaches the Queen-Mother for the nomination of a candidate to fill the vacant stool or the office. The Kurontihene is a liaison between the people and the chief. The Queen-Mother could be the reigning chief's sister or his mother's sister. She knows the history of the genealogy of the members of her clan. It is presumed that she knows all the eligible candidates to the stool. There are always several potential candidates and she has to do some elimination because succession is not by primogeniture. The selection is complicated by the fact that most of the people are convinced that they are eligible if they are in the generational line of succession, and this gives rise to tension and conflict, which sometimes result in protracted litigation.

The Queen Mother, in consultation with the elders of the royal lineage or the 'king-makers', nominates a candidate and informs the Kurontihene accordingly. When the candidate is acceptable, she sends to the father of the candidate, if it is a matrilineal society, to intimate to him the intention of the Queen Mother and her counsellors. After this formality, the Kurontihene informs the young men who then arrest the nominee. He is man-handled and besmeared with white clay, carried shoulder high amidst war songs and paraded through the town from one end to the other. The young men then bring him to the Kurontihene and the priest slaughters a sheep, spilling the blood on his feet while he sits on a sheep's hide. After some formal exchanges, the new chief goes into confinement. During this time, he lives with one of the ritual functionaries who teaches him all the 'wisdom' of chiefship; he is allowed to see visitors. He is taken to the stool house and then presented to the people at a big durbar, where he swears an oath of allegiance and other chiefs reciprocate accordingly. In this ceremony, the chief passes through the three stages of rite-de-passage—separation, segregation and re-integration.

Thus the rituals surrounding the installation of a chief, like other rituals such as the out-dooring of babies and mortuary rites, conform with Van Gennep's concept of social adjustment and integration in the community achieved through rites-de-passage.

The French ethnologist Van Gennep has distinguished them (rites-de-passage) as rites of separation, rites of segregation and rites of integration. Rites of separation express the initiate's relinquishment of his former status. Rites of segregation express the fact that he is now cut off from normal community life. He now occupies no recognized status in society but is, as it were, betwixt and between. Rites of integration express the initiate's acceptance in his new status—adulthood, warriorhood, or whatever it may be—and his re-integration in the community.[9]

Rituals perform certain social needs in the society. They are symbolic expressions of deeper feelings or transcendental ideas of members of a social group. In order to understand the symbolisms of the various behaviour patterns in any given society, it is necessary, and almost mandatory, to understand the social structure of that society. By general consensus among some eminent anthropologists (those of the behaviourist contention) social structure refers to social networks of any society, defined by the articulation of social relationships. Social networks, therefore, define social roles and statuses of individuals in the society. This, of course, is subsumed in most social practices.

For example, rite-de-passage is not merely exotic ritual practices of simple societies which serve as a 'curiosity-trip' for field researchers, but rather an important religious observance with far-reaching social implications. Van Gennep's explanation of rite-de-passage points out the function of this practice in the societies where these rites are observed. The general idea of the ritual is that changes in either natural phenomenon, like change in the lunar system, or in the life of an individual are not taken for granted but are treated with great reverence in the performance of a special ritual. These rites may go on throughout one's life-cycle or may be performed only once or twice. The ritualization of a change in status admits the initiates into the new status. Ritual, therefore, causes rupture in the social network while at the same time creates social integration.

The practice underlines the most important aspect of most non-Western social systems which are by and large highly structured. According to certain ascriptive credentials, individuals fit into a hierarchy and movements either upward or downward the social ladder are determined by certain inherent criteria in the social structure. Members of each class structure should therefore be the same in every respect, and the same is true with the entire community, both the dead and the living.

This is all that lineage values are about. A lineage comprises both the dead and living. This whole idea of ritualization of status may be clearly explained by how the birth of a baby and the rituals which are associated with the happy event are treated.

A new-born baby is not considered a member of the community until its status is ritualized. It is still a member of the spiritual world. Because of its marginal status the mother becomes segregated also. The baby becomes a member after it has severed its membership with the spiritual world by either circumcision or other rites in kind. Gennep calls the period of waiting to be admitted into the community *rite of separation*, and the process of being admitted is referred to as either *rites of orientation or integration*. Every custom that is common among the members of the community into which this baby is being inducted, will be performed for it in order to be fully integrated.

In some instances, the rites are used for class differentation. For example, in certain African countries where most of the educated people are Christians, traditional customs are performed for children of the traditional elites or those of royal or dominant lineage, because of their links with special offices.

Sometimes in an urban setting where it is difficult to distinguish between settlers and indigenous natives, such rituals sort out the people into foreigners and real natives, thus giving the ritual institution certain degree of status symbol. Among the Sierra-Leonians, the Creole or the pu-mui (white man, i.e. an Anglicised native) are identified from the Mende by the various rituals observed among the natives or the indigenous people. (The Creole being freed slaves repatriated to that part of West Africa.)

Kenneth Little in his account of puberty rites among the Mende of Sierra Leone, which is essentially a kind of rite-de-passage, explains the social significance of the ritual in terms of rapid social change and the urbanization process in this part of Africa, says as follows:

> These institutions, as already indicated, are of primary importance in determining ritual behaviour and affecting social attitudes, because the sanctions in nearly every sphere of the common life derive from them. The principal societies involved, in addition to the Poro and the Sande are the Humui, concerned with the general regulation of sexual conduct; the Njayei, concerned with the cure of certain mental conditions and the propagation of agricultural fertility. The Wunde, concerned largely with military training, is popular among the Kpaa Mende, but appears to owe its origin mainly to the Timme neighbours of the latter. These societies are not exclusive, of course, to the Mende, but are shared widely, with the exception of the Wunde, with peoples in Liberia as well as with the adjacent Sherbro, Krim, Gola. (Kenneth L. Little, *The Mende of Sierra Leone*, Routledge & Kegan Paul Ltd., London, p. 240.)

According to Little, there are several secret societies among the Mendes with specific functions. These functions may be economic and social. This is brought out clearly by Firth's concluding paragraph to Kenneth Little's work *The Mende*.

> It is shown how no person can hope to occupy a position of authority in the chiefdom without being a Poro member and receiving Poro support. Even nowadays the Poro seems to play an important role in the election of a chief. The primary function of the Poro is to equip every Mende man for his life as a member of the community. But because its net is so wide the

53

society also has been able to serve as an important regulating force in Mende life and to provide social and ritual ties which cross the boundaries of chiefdoms for political functions. (Ibid., p. 9.)

REFERENCES

1 '... initiation rites are means for the establishment of sexual identity and adult status'. C. Geertz, 'Religion as a Cultural System' in *Anthropological Approach to the Study of Religion*, A.S.A. Monographs 3, Michael Banton (ed.), Tavistock Publications, 1966, p. 2.

2 Piddington, 1950, Vol. I., p. 17.

3 Another tribal group in Ghana—Ga-Adangbe in the Coastal part of Ghana.

4 Piddington, 1950, p. 180.

5 Piddington, 1950, p. 182.

6 There are also descendants from Ashanti, Denkyira and Akwamu.

7 Ayisi, 1965, p. 214.

8 The Kurontihene is next to the Chief in political rank and acts for the chief if he is absent or dead.

9 J. Beattie, *Other cultures*, London: Cohen and West, 1964, p. 211.

VIII

Traditional African Government and Society

THE TERM 'African traditional government' was formerly used to describe a primitive political legacy handed down from a distant past, in primeval times. It presupposed the fact that there were societies bereft of all the sophistication and the machinery of the western type of government, and that there was no efficient means of resolving tensions in the body-politic. Early writers, especially those who were caught up in the mainstream of evolutionary orthodoxy, were misguided about African societies and all human societies, for that matter. Hobbes the seventeenth-century philosopher for example made some crude assumptions about the State. In a conjectural historical analysis, he maintained that civil societies had developed from a 'State of nature', characterized by anarchy and internecine warfare, into a civil society where order and law were maintained by a contract of some kind. Professor Lucy Mair has commented on this Hobbesian theory of the State in her book *Primitive Government* in which she observed

> The seventeenth-century philosopher, Hobbes, contrasted the State of nature in which every man's hand was against his neighbour, with the civil society in which authority had been surrendered to a sovereign ruler.[1]

Hobbes's maintained his theory could be exemplified by the savage people in many places in America. This fallacious assumption was a logical outcome of the evolutionary influence at the time, which made people think of progress as being unilineal. Traditional institutions therefore referred to the beginnings of things in time. Writers, who mostly represented western culture, regarded their societies as having developed from the primitive state in which most societies were still living. Nowadays, the term has acquired a new meaning, it has recaptured the nostalgic spirit of the 'glorious days of the savage' and it means something nobler, something indigenous, peculiar to a people. Tradition is the core of the nascent movement both in Africa and the New World. Black Americans wish to be identified with African tradition in all its aspects, and they feel rather romantic, in a misguided way; the more barbarous and bizarre they look the more African they feel ... for Africans were believed to be barbarous.

We therefore mean by 'traditional government' the indigenous African ways of government, without any implication of crudeness in the system. It will refer to the pre-colonial era, when the African peoples managed their own affairs and administered justice among themselves. In attempting to do this we must pay attention to previous books on this matter. We draw inspiration from writers like Professor M. Fortes, M. Gluckman, E. E. Evans-Pritchard and others who embarked on a most fruitful exploration into the field of comparative politics. In their book, *African Political Systems*, their predominant concern was explicit from the beginning.

'We have not found that the theories of political philosophers have helped us to understand the societies we have studied and we consider them of a little scientific value, for their conclusions are seldom formulated in terms of observed behaviour capable of being tested by this criterion. Political philosophy has chiefly concerned itself with how men ought to live and what form of government they ought to have, rather than what are their political habits and institutions.'[2]

The authors were therefore concerned with description and classification of political institutions. The authors of *African Political Systems* described and distinguished two main political organizations and categorized them into Groups A and B respectively.

Radcliffe-Brown in his introduction to the book defined political organization as follows:

In studying political organization, we have to deal with the maintenance or establishment of social order within a territorial framework, by the organized exercise of coercive authority through the use or possibility of use of physical force. In well organized states, the police and the army are the instruments by which coercion is exercised.[3]

It is necessary to look at the different systems of political organization which are found in traditional Africa. The early anthropologists distinguished and described two types of political systems.

Group A consists of those societies which have centralized authority, administrative machinery and judicial institutions —in short a government—in which cleavages of wealth, privilege, and status correspond to the distribution of power and authority. This group is exemplified by societies such as the Zulu, the Ngwato, the Bemba and Ashanti.[4]

In this group the writers have mainly been concerned with the description of governmental organization, such as an account of the status of kings and classes and the roles of administrative officials of one kind or another. They also deal with the privileges of rank, the differences in wealth and power, the regulation of tax and tribute, the territorial divisions of the state and their relation to the central authority. In short, it is an account of the social and political structure.

Group B deals with societies which are uncentralized or acephalous societies.

This consists of those societies which lack centralized authority, administrative machinery and constituted judicial institutions. In short, they lack government. This group comprises such people as the Logoli, the Tallensi and the Nuer.[5]

It is a rather curious hypothesis to advance that because these societies lack modern governmental paraphernalia, they lack government of any kind.

There is a third type described by the contributors to *African Political Systems*, which is exemplified by the Bushmen, where the largest political unit embraces people, all of whom are inter-related by kinship so that 'political relations are co-terminous with kinship relations and the political structure and kinship organization are completely fused.'

There is also in East Africa, among the Nilo-Hamitic speaking peoples, another type of political system. In this system, political relations are controlled by the holders of statuses or age-sets.

We shall now look closely at the various systems and analyse their functions by 'structural-functional' analysis. We shall look at some of the problems facing those placed in authority. Every person in every society has to conform to certain cultural rules or regulations. Since for order to be maintained a certain degree of predictability in behaviour patterns is needed, A must be able to anticipate the reaction of B in a given social situation. Deviations from accepted rules of behaviour are checked by sanctions in the societies, and the enforcement of sanctions is the work of special officers in the more complex centralized societies.

In simple societies where there is no judicial authority, law and justice take different forms. Private wrongs are avenged by private individuals and any of their friends whom they can get to help them to resist attack or to help attack, to defend or offend. This is true of the Zabramas of Northern Ghana. When a Zabrama sees a friend being attacked he puts down whatever he may be carrying and he grabs a stick to help him. At this stage, the method of redress is not organized, it is haphazard. Hobhouse analyses it in the following way:

> The growth of law and justice is pretty closely connected
> in its several stages with the forms of social organization ...
> Private wrongs are revenged by private individuals, and
> anyone whom they can get to help them ... But even at a very
> low stage, this uncertain and fitful action begins to take more
> definite shape. There are two possible lines of development.
> On the one hand, the method of self-redress may be
> organized and reduced to a system under a regular code
> of recognized custom. On the other hand, the maintenance
> of order, the settlement of disputes, the punishment of
> offences, and the redress of wrongs may be undertaken
> partially or completely, as the case may be, by the community
> acting through a regularly constituted organ for administration
> of justice.[6]

At this level of social development custom may prescribe certain methods of administering justice so that punishment is not in excess of offence. The simplest form of such rules is the Mosaic. Law (Lex Talionis) 'an eye for an eye and a tooth for a tooth'.

> The simplest and earliest of those rules is the famous Lex Talionis ... familiar to us from the chapter of Exodus, but far earlier than Exodus in its first formulation. We find it, like many other primitive rules of law, in the recently discovered code of King Hammurabi which is earlier than the Book of the Covenant perhaps by 1300 years ... We find it applicable to body injuries, to breaches of the marriage laws ... In some cases the idea of exact retaliation is carried out with the utmost literalness—sometimes as when a man who has killed another by falling on him from a tree is himself put to death by the same method.[7]

From this type of individual vengeance, we find a system of almost organized vengeance. This is exemplified by the administration of justice in societies which lack the modern paraphernalia of social control.

An example of an acephalous society combining some of these methods is provided by the Nuer of the Southern Sudan as they were described by Evans-Pritchard thirty years ago. Their social structure is organized on a segmentary basis and each segment is autonomous—this segment may constitute a small group of a village or may be a whole village. Each individual's interest is jealously safe-guarded by his kin-group and any injury to an individual is revenged by the victim with the backing of his kin group.

There are various offences and each offence has its appropriate redress. Stealing is redressed by direct restitution. If someone steals cattle from a person of an outside group, the cattle of the thief and his kinsmen are open to a threat of being seized by any of the victim's kinsmen who happen to set eyes on any cattle of the offending group. Social contact is suspended temporarily under such conditions.

Lucy Mair describes the state of hostility in her book as a 'state of quarantine'. In cases of homicide, the whole kin group of the murderer is open to threat of death in the hands of the victim's kin-group.

When a man had been killed, it was believed to be dangerous
for his lineage and that of the killer to come into contact.
This condition of ritual danger was created automatically
by the act of killing.[8]

The only way of obviating this danger is to appeal to a ritual
functionary known as the leopard-skin chief, and it is this ritual
functionary alone who can remove the blood feud which might
break out. This is done by payment in kind.

But the Nuer agreed that a feud could be brought to an end
by the offer of a payment of cattle in compensation for an
offence and by a formal ceremony of reconciliation.[9]

The Tallensi in Northern Ghana are another example of a society
of this type. In this society a *tendaana*, Custodian of the Earth, is
primarily a religious functionary. His office is homologous with
chiefship, but oriented towards the Earth. He 'prospers' the community by ensuring the Earth's beneficence. His ritual relationship
with the Earth imposes certain taboos (e.g. he may never wear
cloth, but only skins) and enables him to accept the responsibility
of dealing directly with it. Hence all lost property, not the pre-
rogative of chiefs, must be delivered to a tendaana. Lest the earth
be offended, a tendaana must pierce the soil for a new grave and
turn the first sod for making a farm or building a homestead on
virgin land. Portions of the animals sacrificed on such occasions
belong to him. Tendaanas may not sell men, but if a chief sold a
vagrant person, he would give a cow to the tendaana of the area
where the man was found as a piacular offering to the Earth.
Because the Earth abhors bloodshed, tendaanas have ritual power
to stop fighting and to mediate in disputes. The tendaanas perform
the sacrifices offered to the earth to expiate murder. Their curse
or blessing is more potent than a chief's since the earth is universal
and can punish or bless a man anywhere.

In a centralized society, the settlement of disputes and offences
is straightforward because there are definite processes, judicial
machinery and the police to cope with such offences. The traditional procedure, however, is not along the lines of modern judi-
ciary. The chief and his counsellors constitute courts of justice,

and the method adopted is the *modus vivendi* method—discussion and exchange of views affecting a particular issue until unanimity has been reached. Essentially, however, the method is the same as the Western type of administration of justice.

The Ashantis in Ghana are an example of a centralized system of government. Political authority is vested in the Asantehene and his subordinate chiefs. The Ashanti system has been adopted by other states which used to have different systems. For example, the tribes in Akwapim have formed themselves into a federation based on the Akan system of government with a military posture. The Akwapim state is neither kin-based nor symbolized in any kind of supernatural concepts; it happened to be established for pragmatic reasons. The reorganization of congeries of tribes which were hitherto autonomous social groups into a single fighting unit was necessary for the effective defence of a newly formed state and also for the consolidation of the power of the new 'alien' paramount chief.

After the various formalities for the setting up of the state had been finalised, Safori, the new paramount chief, started a process of 'akanization'.[10] The structure of the new political system took the form of a military organization and Safori flanked each one of the seventeen towns with a special representative of his tribe. The representatives so elected were given the titles of 'Amankrados' or 'Osomanyawa', meaning deputies of the paramountcy.

The structure of the divisional chieftaincy is hierarchical. A number of chiefs are given the title of divisional chief and are assigned to various divisions in the state according to their ethnic origins. These chiefs enjoy a degree of political autonomy in some matters but in others they are expected to consult the paramount chief and his elders. The elders of the paramount chief constitute another separate structure outside the divisional system, delicately linked with the divisional system so that there is a happy co-ordination between the paramount chief and the individual chiefs through the members of the special political structure who are chiefs in their own right. Akwapim statecraft, though not like the Western system, has some of the sophistication of Western democracies. The chiefs are then the focal points of the political system. They constitute the back-bone of the body politic.

IDEALS OF CHIEFTAINSHIP

Like all institutions, chieftainship is controlled by certain un-written laws. These ensure the security of chieftainship and at the same time render it most vulnerable. The whole procedural arrange-ments which precede the installation of a person into the office of chief are so complex and so moving that any individual who passes through the complete ritual acquires an air of mystique associated with the office he occupies. At the same time, all the people who participate in such rites acquire a sense of communion with mystical forces which lift them out of themselves into the world of an-cestral spirits.

A chief is a hallowed person. No action that has any element of opprobrium should be committed by a chief. Most of these actions may be classified as sinful actions. Chiefs should not engage in adulterous practices or incestuous congresses, stealing, sorcery or kindred actions. A chief found guilty of any of these actions or offences may be liable to destoolment. Some of the virtues expected of chiefs are generosity, kindness, humility, respect for elders, fecundity and respect for ancestral spirits. These virtues may be found in some chiefs, nevertheless, they are virtues which are hard to come by. In every respect, people expect these virtues from their chief, for they heap adulations on him and make pretensions for him which he will never achieve.

The ideal chief is different from the real chief, thus there is always the chief as he is, and the chief as his people want him to be. These two images of a chief, that he has of himself and that which his people have of him are the sources of most political tensions and troubles in the political structure.

Every chief is held in honour by all the people: He is called 'Nana' which means 'grandfather'. This title symbolizes the fact that he represents the ancestral spirits. All chiefs are said to be divine, and the external symbols of their divinity are expressed in various taboos.

(a) A chief is not supposed to eat food prepared by a
    menstruating woman.

(b) Whenever a chief sees a corpse, he has to submit to special ritual purification.
(c) A chief is not expected to stumble or kick a stone or slip and fall down. Any such incident requires special ritual purification.
(d) A chief is not expected to go anywhere unaccompanied.

The changes which are occurring in traditional societies are affecting both the structure of chieftainship and the values attached to this sacred institution. Most of the occupants of the office of chieftainship are now educated and contaminated by Western ideas, so that they look at the institution as an office which places them above others. Social prestige and economic interests—where these interests exist—are the main incentives for the assumption of the office. Where economic interests are poor, some chiefs combine normal occupations in the government with chieftainship so that the office has lost its aura of mystique and most chiefs have changed their traditional style of life.

REFERENCES

1 Lucy Mair, *Primitive Government*. Penguin Books, 1964.
2 Fortes and Evans-Pritchard (eds.), 1940, p. 4.
3 A. E. Radcliffe-Brown, *African Political Systems*, Fortes and Evans-Pritchard, (eds.), 1940, p. xiv.
4 Fortes and Evans-Pritchard, (eds.), 1940, 'Introduction', p. 5.
5 Fortes and Evans-Pritchard, (eds.), 1940, p. 5.
6 L. T. Hobhouse, *Morals in Evolution*, London: 1951 edition, pp. 71-2.
7 Hobhouse, 1951, p. 74.
8 Mair, 1964, p. 105.
9 Mair, 1964, p. 105.
10 This term refers to the process of introducing the Akan culture—the acculturation of the Guans and the Kyerepongs.

IX

Akan Judicial Processes

THE OATH system is crucial to Akan judicial processes. Unlike Western judicial systems, cases of breach of norms and social behaviour are brought to the notice of chiefs by invoking the force of the oath to determine whether a breach has been committed and, if so, how to arrive at an amicable settlement. The oath is a recitation of a customary statement which is legally binding on the one who recites it and on the man against whom the oath is sworn. The legal force of the oath is homologous to a bench warrant and its caveat can only be exercised by the chief who has power over the oath. It is his oath (*Ohene Ntam*). The statement contained in the oath recalls some historical event, war, defeat or the death of an important chief. The chief is reminded of the history of his ancestors and these oaths refer to events in their history.

In some African societies there are regularized means of determining whether a breach has been committed. Dr P. H. Gulliver in his book on social control observes:

> In every society there must, by definition, exist regularized
> procedures which can be used to deal with alleged breaches
> of norms and injuries they cause; there must be ways by
> which it can be established whether in fact a breach has
> occurred and what is the extent of the injuries and there
> must be means of determining and enforcing decisions which
> provide a settlement of the dispute and perhaps also means
> which tend to prevent a recurrence of the matter. In some
> societies, of course, the principal means to these ends are
> contained in the complex of political authorities, police
> courts, judges, lawyers and code of laws.[1]

Of course, Gulliver was describing a quasi-Westernized society with a developed judicial system. In an African judicial system bereft of all this judicial paraphernalia, justice is administered differently.

In Ashanti with a quasi-judiciary, the oath is used for seeking redress of infractions of the social norms. The Ashantis have two categories of oath systems—*Ntankese* (big oath) and *Ntam* (ordinary oath). In Akwapim, the great oath is known as *Wukuda ne Sokodei* or the Oath of Wednesday and Sokodei. (Sokodei is a town in Anwona, Eastern Ghana, where the Akwapim fought against the Anwonas and where they lost many of their celebrated men). The oath is sworn when one wants to have an offence redressed by the Omanhene, or any other chief, depending on the type of oath sworn. In the long run, however, everyone in Akwapim, chiefs and commoners, come under the oath of the Omanhene; in other words, the whole of the State comes within his jurisdiction.

The oath is also sworn by newly elected chiefs to declare their loyalty to other chiefs, ancestors and their people. As I have already stated, all public delicts are brought to a chief's court by means of the oath system.

Kofi Nnam swears an oath on Kwadwo Botwe in the following manner 'Meka Wukuda ne Sokodei se me sika eyeme no wo Kwadwo Botwe na wofae, enti se woamma yeanko Omanhene anim ankokyere me ase a, woto ntam'.[2] The English rendering of the oath is as follows: 'I swear the oath of Wednesday and Sokodei that my money which got lost, you Kwadwo Botwe stole it, therefore if you do not come with me to the Omanhene's presence to explain this theft, you have violated the oath I have sworn'. Kofi Nnam may also swear the same oath to declare his innocence, but whatever is the case these two men are taken by a third person in whose presence the oath is sworn. This is called *Kyere-dedua* or warrant arrest.

The person or persons who happen to be there when the oath is sworn demand a warrant fee called *apaasobode* before the defendant and the plaintiff are taken by him or them to the chief. This fee is not fixed, because mileages are charged besides the customary twelve shillings payable as a stamp fee on the payment of the warrant fee. This stamp fee is called *Ntampiade*. After the fees have been paid, the oath swearers have to find sureties when they are taken to the chief's court. If the case is heard on the same day, sureties may not be necessary. Usually, a day is fixed to enable the chief to convene a meeting of all his elders who have to advise him during the hearing of the suit. When these various formalities are gone through, a day is fixed by the chief for the money to be paid by the person or persons who have brought the oath swearers.

The oath system turns all adult males in a chiefdom into a voluntary police service, for any person can arrest defaulters of an oath to the chief and a small amount is paid for the performance of one's duty. The paying of the fee by the swearer of the oath confirms his intentions and it gives the oath a legal force. The oath system facilitates the judicial processes and it transcends territorial boundaries. If someone, even in another chiefdom, swears the oath of a chief it is like an appeal to Caesar. The chief of the same chiefdom will look into the case and make preliminary investigations and then he will send the persons involved to the chief whose oath has been sworn.

Not all cases are taken to the chief personally. Though the chief has the right to undo an oath, that is, to nullify its efficacy, certain councillors of the chief may settle matters involving the chief's oath and report decisions to the chief (and the payments made in such matters). Fines are arbitrarily fixed in most cases, but there are certain offences which have fixed fines. In most societies fines are fixed in relation to the gravity of the offence and its nature.

TYPES OF OFFENCES

Busia, following Radcliffe-Brown's analysis of offences in traditional societies, distinguished between civil offences and private offences respectively—public delict and private delict.

> The Ashanti themselves divided offences into two categories. Those which did not concern the chief, that is the central authorities, but were household cases (*afisem*) and those which concerned the central authority because they were taboos or things hated by the tribe (*Oman akyiwade*).[3]

Offences which come under the category of *Oman akyiwade* should go before the chief at all costs and according to Rattray, on whose work Busia based his analysis, the *Oman akyiwade* are classified as follows:

    i. murder
   ii. suicide
  iii. certain sexual offences
  iv. certain forms of abuse
   v. certain kinds of assault
  vi. certain kinds of stealing
 vii. the invocation of a curse upon a chief
viii. treason and cowardice
  ix. witchcraft
   x. the violation of any other recognized taboo
  xi. breaking of a law or command enjoined by the swearing
     of an oath.

Rattray himself distinguished between what were regarded as offences against the State and those against private individuals.[4] The important thing to realize is that the Ashanti do not treat all offences as offences against the whole community. I found in my field work among the Akwapim that they had three rather than two categories of offences. I discovered that the two categories of offences discussed by both Rattray and Busia do not encompass all the offences which the Akwapim had to settle. There were conflicts which affected the social structure *per se* and there were two others which were restricted to the household or between lineage groups. The different offences were dealt with in somewhat different ways as I describe in the following passages:

All quarrels are settled by moot, and the constitution of each moot varies inversely with the nature of the dispute, and it also reflects the seriousness of such a dispute. When the dispute in question is a private delict, the members of the moot are selected from the household and such settlement is called 'Afisiesie' 'repairing the household'. If it is a social delict then the moot is large and external for members consist not only of elders from the ward but also of independent elders from neighbouring wards, who are invited to help to settle such a dispute. Such a settlement is called 'Abusuasem' —'lineage or clan case'. On the other hand all cases involving an infringement of the chief's oath are heard by the chief and his councillors or by the chief's representatives.[5]

The final type of case I refer to as public delict or *Amansem*, a litigation affair. It is usually settled in the chief's court or his nominee's house.

ARBITRATION

The commonest method of settling conflicts between two persons is by arbitration—the method whereby one person or a group of persons are invited to adjudicate cases of interpersonal conflict. Arbitration is always held with the consent of the persons involved in the conflict, for it is only then that settlement can be achieved. If one of the persons chooses, he may refuse to have the case settled in that way. Third-party intervention is therefore one of the features of the judicial system in some parts of Africa. This, of course, will appear strange to the Western mind used to inter-personal conflicts being settled by the simple agreement of the persons concerned. Arbitration, by and large, has no legal force for verdicts from these quasi-courts, or *ad hoc* courts, may be challenged by one of the parties and the case may be taken to a proper court. In some cases, however, verdicts at arbitration are given legal confirmation by the chief's court where a *prima facie* case has been established and there is uncertainty about the appropriate fine. Men who are invited to serve as arbitrators are usually men of some social standing in the society and in some cases they are counsellors to the chief. When such personalities are involved in arbitration, the verdict is seldom challenged. When the case is taken to the chief's court after it has been settled by counsellors of a chief, the result of the case will not be different because the counsellor who has already heard the case will influence the decision at that level too. Anyone can take a case to be settled by arbitration—household cases, marital conflicts, simple quarrels between brothers and disputes between friends. Arbitration helps people to establish a *prima facie* case in disputes because at these quasi-courts they are to state their case and get all the necessary guidance and if they should decide to take the case further, they have all the evidence to support it.

In arbitration a person's social status is taken into account when verdicts are given. If the people who are involved in the dispute are of equal social status then strict impartiality is enforced, but if one of the parties stands in an asymmetrical relation to another, then the person of a higher rank comes off better, because it is not proper to ask a person of a higher rank to apologise to a person of a lower rank. In all arbitrations which involve persons of high social status, the arbitrators do exercise discretionary powers by intervening personally, and in this case none of the parties is blamed. The chief arbitrator says: 'I have put my foot on the matter 'matu menan asi asem no so.' Fines at arbitrations should not be too heavy. The members of the panel have to share part of the fine. Nowadays, chiefs have been divested of the judicial functions they once had, and all the cases which come before them are of the nature of arbitration settlements.

In other parts of Africa it has been established that arbitration is more institutionalized in respect to the structure of the panel, qualifications of persons who should constitute a panel and the types of cases which should go before these arbitrators. In Tivland, situated on either side of the Benue River in Northern Nigeria, the judicial process is handled and controlled by special people in the community by virtue of certain social criteria. These men by their very nature exert strong influence on the community so that they also constitute symbols of sanctions in the judicial system *per se*. Laura Bohannan's account of these people and their political system is illuminating. According to her there are two sets of personalities involved in the judicial process, namely Elders and Men of Prestige. Men of Prestige (Shaba) and Elders (Vesen) wield wide influence in the society because of their positions in the social structure. The Elders are usually the oldest men in the society and they constitute a gerontocratic core of the political structure. They are the heads of the compound, the centre of all conflicts and tension, which if not controlled, filtrate into other parts of the society. They are endowed, it is believed, with certain innate qualities, such as to give them the necessary political and legal competence to settle disputes. An Elder, according to Laura Bohannan, possesses

i. knowledge of jural custom and of the genealogical and personal histories of his agnates; ii. the mastery of health and fertility granting magic (Akombo); iii. the personality and ability which in Tiv eyes mark the possession of witchcraft substance (tsaw) ... A man of Prestige, on the other hand, is a man whose wealth, generosity and astuteness give him certain influence over people and formerly allowed the purchase of slaves and thus the formation of a 'gang' to furnish safe-conduct to those strangers who paid tribute and to rob those who did not. These men then had a certain measure of physical force (no longer available to them) at their command. Unless they were elders, however, they were ultimately controllable by the powers of witch-craft and magic lying within the hands of that gerontocracy.[6]

The two groups of people in the society can in this way complement each other's qualities and they, in concerted action, control the whole community. Tension between these groups of men may be reflected in the society and create a state of anomie, therefore care is taken that they operate in the strictest agreement and amity. Cases go before them by certain prescribed procedures either in the form of a moot (Jir) or inquest. The moot is usually selected according to kinship ties and members of common agnatic ties could serve on a moot. The system of the Tiv judicial system is similar to the Akan in many ways, but not in the selection of the arbitrators, their qualifications and the period of appointment of such people. Among the Akan, membership of the arbitration panel is by temporary appointment, similar to serving on a jury. From the above, it may be concluded that the system of arbitration is crucial to the administration of justice in most African societies, and it facilitates, and in fact speeds up, settlement of potential conflicts and resolves tensions in the body politic.

REFERENCES

1 P. H. Gulliver, *Social Control in an African Society*, Routledge and Kegan Paul, Boston University Press, 1963, p. 7.

2 Safori Fianko, *Tivifo Amammuisem*, Macmillan, 1950, p. 27.

3 Busia, 1951, p. 66.

4 See R. S. Rattray, *Ashanti Law and Constitution*, London: Oxford University Press, 1950, for full treatment of this topic.

5 Ayisi, 1965, p. 377.

6 L. Bohannan, 'Political Aspects of Tiv Social Organization' in *Tribes Without Rulers: Studies in African Segmentary Systems*, J. Middleton and D. Tait (eds.), Routledge and Kegan Paul, 1958, p. 55.

X

African Religion

SOCIOLOGISTS AND social anthropologists have treated African religion
as if it were a bizarre museum item entirely different from other
religious phenomena found in Western culture. They have given
it a conceptual interpretation that betrays their prejudices about
African cultures, which in many ways are not valid and lack
rational justification.[1] There has been too much confused thinking
about the religious practices and beliefs of Africans. Africans have
been described by some writers as pagans, heathens or men whose
lives are dominated and trammelled by superstitions. It has been
said that they lack any theological ideas and that all the elements
which make Judaism, Islam or Christianity sublime are lacking in
African religion. People who should have known better, especially
missionaries, were completely misguided about African religion,
and by their muddled thinking propagated erroneous ideas about
African religious beliefs.

Evans-Pritchard in his book *Theories of Primitive Religion*,
devoted a chapter to what he describes as 'the great mythmakers'.
He begins with Darwin, the founder of the evolutionary theory,
and goes on to discuss Marx, Engels, Freud and Frazer. These men
were not only dismissing in a perfunctory manner primitive religion as mere 'epiphenomenal essences', but were using what they
called 'primitive religion' as a paradigm to justify their attack on
religion *per se*. Their methodology was essentially evolutionary.
Society was said to have been gradually moving towards a scientific
consciousness after which religion would be entirely discarded. But
the main contention of most writers on religion was that primitive
religion lacked theological awareness. Evans-Pritchard writing
about this attitude towards 'primitive religion' re-appraised Sir
Samuel Baker's *obiter dicta* in the following pungent words:

I give an example from a region with which I am well
acquainted. In view of recent papers and extensive monographs

on the religion of the Northern Nilotes it is strange to read what a famous explorer, Sir Samuel Baker, said then in his address to the Ethnological Society of London in 1866. "Without any exception, they are without a belief in a Supreme Being. Neither have they any form of worship nor idolatry nor is the darkness of their minds enlightened by even a ray of superstition. The mind is as stagnant as the morass which forms its puny world".[2]

Baker's view is obviously wrong and is not tenable in the light of present evidence of religion in African cultures.

The problem with the sociology of religion is that very few writers have shown any sustained interest in the subject and those who have been interested have either been critical of the whole idea of religion or they have been people with the best intentions, but strangers to the cultures they studied; therefore they had no insight into the deeper meanings of the religions of the people they studied. They also held concepts foreign to cultures other than their own and in using these concepts carried within them some of the connotations which these terms conveyed.

The most influential writers on primitive religion are Tylor, who was brought up as a Quaker; Frazer, a Presbyterian; Marett in the Church of England; Malinowski, a Catholic; while Durkheim, Levy-Bruhl and Freud had Jewish backgrounds. But as Evans-Pritchard reminds us, these men at the time of writing were attempting to justify their loss of faith in their religions. Everything they said and wrote on primitive religion was flavoured with their early religious training and subsequent experiences. They were not on sure ground as far as religion was concerned because they had lost their faith and were concerned with religious practices rather than the spiritual content of these beliefs. What they had to say, however, has served as working hypotheses for subsequent writers.

Religious practices were neatly categorized by these writers, and Tylor for example described and distinguished two forms of religious practices—animism and naturalism. Animism is believed to occur 'at the threshold of conceptual thinking' and 'in the absence of any rigid distinctions between the natural and the supernatural, the animate and the inanimate, the phenomenal order is identified with that of human existence and the behaviour of the

72

one equated with that of the other'.[3] Tylor's theory stresses the idea of the soul or ghost and extends this to animate creatures and inanimate things. The theory may be broken down into two main theses. The first has to do with origin and the second with development. With these models, he maintained that primitive man's reflection on such experiences as death, disease, trances, visions and above all dreams, substantiated the postulate of the duality of human nature and personality. Since the soul lives in the body it can detach itself from the body. The temporary abdication of the soul from the body and the experiences outside the body as exemplified by dreams, trances, visions and death led Tylor and his supporters to develop the 'ghost theory'. Tylor came to the conclusion that 'some immaterial entity, the soul' can leave the body at night and wander at will. At death it leaves the body permanently (the basis of the ancestor cult). Then the worship of natural objects arises from potency as observed by Professor E. O. James:

As animistic and polytheistic ideas develop, the process of personification includes a great variety of modes of expression with clearly defined anthropomorphic, theriomorphic or naturalistic forms unlike the shadowy and vaguely conceived potencies and providences of more rudimentary phases of culture. Thus, in contrast to the Numina of Roman religion, the Greek pantheon presents us with an organized world of deities with outstanding personalities and attributes while the ancient Egyptians represented their gods either in human guise ... or as animals ... and sometimes in a combination of the two.[4]

The worship of natural objects was born.

Another interesting writer is Sir James Frazer, who wrote about magic and religion, and according to whose thesis religion grew out of magic. Frazer, like the other writers, was describing religious rites, yet confused this with religious beliefs. He tried to show that magic was a mistaken application of the principle or laws of association which scientists used for interpreting natural phenomena. He observed:

73

The fatal flaw of magic lies, not in its general assumption
of the sequence of events determined by law, but in its
total misconception of the particular laws which govern
that sequence ... The principles of association are excellent
in themselves and, indeed, absolutely essential to the working
of the human mind. Legitimately applied, they yield magic,
the bastard child of science.[5]

There were two types of magic according to Frazer—homoeopathic magic and contagious magic. Homoeopathic magic depended
on the theory that similar objects with common characteristics
affect one another, so one can influence another person by initiating
this effect with an object similar in appearance to that person. Lucy
Mair puts the point more clearly:

The classic example is sticking pins into an image of
somebody you dislike. Sorcery takes this form. Contagious
magic is the use of anything belonging to a person one
dislikes to cause the person harm; for example, his hair
or nail clipping.[6]

Frazer was, in fact, describing certain rites and not religious beliefs.
These rites are not religious because there is behind them no theological belief. They have been improvised by men hoping to induce
or bring into action certain powerful forces which would produce
a desired effect. There is a distinction between these rites and those
that are intended for the Supreme Being.

I want now to discuss Emile Durkheim who treated religion as
a social fact, re-vitalizing the social sentiments. He rejected the
theories of other writers before him and wrote:

We propose to study the most primitive and simple religion
which is actually known, found in a society whose organization
is surpassed by none in its simplicity.[7]

He, therefore, selected for his study, by secondary sources, the
Arunta, an Australian tribe:

The life of the Arunta was sharply divided into secular

74

pursuits of scattered small groups (uniform, languishing
and dull) and the sacred periodic collective gatherings of
the clan marked by exaltation, group euphoria, and even
the breaking of taboos.[8]

Durkheim saw these collective activities as the 'birth place of
religious sentiments and ideas' and from this he developed the
social fact theory of religion, i.e. religious beliefs originate in social
groupings and reflect the power of society. Durkheim based his
hypothesis on the religious practices of the Arunta and the totemic
groupings of these rather outlandish people tucked away in a far
corner of the world—Australia. The weakness of Durkheim's
theory of religion lies in the fact that it does not refer to any
theological ideas, nor does it pretend to imply the existence of a
Supreme Being in primitive religion and this has been the source
of a kind of orthodoxy in the anthropological analysis of primitive
religion by many writers. From the time of Durkheim's classic
book on religion, anthropologists have placed too much premium
on religious rites[9] and have even gone so far as to say religion is
the rationalization of these bizarre practices which were naïve in-
terpretations of man's ideas of himself, the world and the universe.
This orthodoxy has sterilized the development of a sound sociological treatment of the history of religion. For example, witchcraft
and sorcery are categorized as religious practices. Sorcery, and the
same goes for witchcraft, does not form a part of the system of
beliefs which Africans regard as religious. Both witchcraft and
sorcery are regarded as reprehensible and anti-social and the rites
which magicians perform are mundane and improvised. *Odutofo*,
which in Akan refers to a sorcerer, is a condemnatory term. Idiom-
atically it means a murderer and it is naïve and ludicrous to describe
it as religious.

We turn now to another French writer, Levy-Bruhl, who also
stressed the relationship of religion to the social structure. His
thesis is valid in as far as he maintains that religious beliefs were
the product of the social milieu of the people:

The mentality of the individual is derived from the
collective representations of his society, which are obligatory
for him and these representations are functions of institutions.

Consequently certain types of representations and therefore certain ways of thinking belong to certain types of social structure.[10]

But the argument breaks down when it concludes that peoples of simple technology have a 'primitive' or 'pre-logical mentality'. Levy-Bruhl was wrong in distinguishing degrees of religious experience by the paradigms of social development. Religious beliefs are a matter of common human experience. The problems which evoke such experience and the available apparatus for dealing with these problems at human levels would determine which of these problems should be passed on for religious treatment. Ginsberg rightly observes in discussing Hobhouse's ideas:

At the core of the religious consciousness there are, Hobhouse thinks, elements of genuine experience giving true insight into the real. The experience, however, is never merely intellectual, but is permanently rooted in emotional needs. Man requires to be reconciled to his place in nature. He needs guidance in action, consolation in grief, fortitude in bearing irreparable loss. In varying ways, religions hold out hope of complete and abiding satisfaction. But they do not build this hope on any empirical investigation of the conditions of such satisfaction.[11]

Primitive people as well as people of advanced cultures are predisposed to these experiences at various times and when in moments of exaltation, distress or debasement, they seek solace or expression of their feelings, it is only to a Supreme Being, above ordinary experience, that they turn. African religion does not, therefore, lack theological sovereignty and there is a clear distinction between ideas relating to the Supreme Being and other deities. As Busia says, in speaking of the Ashanti:

Though Ashanti religious ceremonials concern these intermediary deities and the spirits of the ancestors, the people have a feeling of awe and veneration for the Supreme Being who is high above all deities and who animates them all.[12]

Rites are, therefore, mnemonics of systems of religious procedures for reaching the incomprehensible.

Another example of this type of confusion is seen in discussions of the ancestor cult. There has been a heated controversy on this subject. Some writers treat this as peculiar to African culture, but others have expressed a different view. One writer says:

> The ancient Greeks appear to have had elaborate cults concerned with beliefs about ghosts and shades, but no ancestor cult.[13]

This contention is challenged by the statement by Radcliffe-Brown:

> A most important part of the religion of ancient Greece and Rome was the worship of ancestors ... A religious cult of the same general kind has existed in China from ancient times to the present day. Cults of the same kind exist today and can be studied in many parts of Africa and Asia.[14]

The ancestor cult prescribes appropriate rites for contact with ancestors and the spirit world. The cult does not replace religion, *per se*, in these societies. They are the means by which belief in life after death is indicated and as Busia observed, 'whose constant contact with the life of man on the earth brings the world of spirits so close to the land of the living.'[15]

Both Radcliffe-Brown and Fortes share the view that the ancestor cult is a universal religious phenomenon:

> There is a general agreement that wherever it occurs, ancestor worship is rooted in domestic kinship, and descent relations and institutions.[16]

It may be inferred that wherever there are small descent groups, ancestor worship may be found.

I will now go on to sum up some of the crucial problems brought into focus by the preceding discussion. My thesis is that religious beliefs are essentially about a Creator, Supreme Being, and that rites are means of establishing contact with this Being. Religious beliefs are therefore endemic phenomena and they are different from mundane procedures improvised by magicians. Although I am not prepared to go all the way with Frazer by saying that religion developed from magic, the 'bastard science', I am prepared to say that religious rites are only means for reaching the spirit world. The spirit world is inhabited by spirits and it is believed to be organized on a hierarchical structure with a Supreme Being at the top. Busia describes the Ashanti system in the following words:

There is the Great Spirit, the Supreme Being who
created all things and who manifests his power through
a pantheon of gods; below these are lesser spirits which
animate trees, animals or charms. Then there are the
ever-present spirits of the ancestors (nsamanfo) whose
constant contact with the life of man on the earth brings
the world of the spirits so close to the land of the living.[17]

Abraham also, in *The Mind of Africa* puts this idea succinctly about the Akan state:

The Akan state was a sacred state in the sense that
it was conceived as falling inside a world inhabited by
human beings as well as spirits and gods to whom human
beings owed specific duties discharged through appropriate
rites and with whom human beings were in constant
communion on the grounds of kinship.[18]

It is believed that some of the spirits in the spirit world are ancestors with whom some people have had personal experiences during the earthly life and whom they could contact by performing appropriate rites. These spirits by virtue of their changed status in the society, having gone into higher realms, are endowed with supernatural powers and they live in the 'shade' of the Almighty Supreme Being, Onyankopon, interceding and supplicating on the behalf of the living, helping where they can and enlisting the assistance of the Supreme Being when they are incapable of helping. Sometimes groups of ancestral spirits coalesce to help in crises. The Akans even distinguish between ancestral spirits—

regarding them as structured in a hierarchical organization. Belief in the class-structured system of the spirit world is reflected in the social fields with appropriate rituals for different deities on different occasions.

This idea of life in the spirit world and the interest of the ancestral spirits in the world of the living is demonstrated in mortuary rites. When a relative dies, he or she is buried by close kinsmen who, as part of the rites, present the deceased with money for the journey into the spirit world and give messages to departed relatives. On this occasion all sorts of messages are sent through this person. This means that religious rites which serve as means of contacting the spirit world are abandoned in favour of personal messages. This is like sending letters to a friend or relative abroad through another person rather than through the the post. The messages take the form of supplications and they are intended to influence the ancestral spirits to be beneficent. The thesis that the ancestor cult is an end in itself and that the worship has as its main objective an adulation of the spirits is not only fallacious, but naïve. The Akans believe in a Supreme Being and ancestral spirits are a way to reach that Being. Abraham takes a positive stand on the importance of a Supreme Being in Akan cosmological belief. He observes:

God himself was well to the fore of Akan thinking.
He luxuriated in various by-names of which Onyame seems
to be central. Quite a few writers, Westermann, Rattray,
and latterly Meyerowitz among them have sought to identify
Onyame or Nyame as a sky-god because of a supposed
etymology.[19]

The Supreme Being is made up of a duality—male and female—and this is consistent with the idea of fertility and bountifulness associated with Onyame. The Supreme Being is not human and he is considered beneficent. The ancestral spirits having once been human have human attributes of jealousy, selfishness and love and can be invoked to meet certain of our needs, but with the permission of the Supreme Being. The Akans in religious practices and beliefs use special appellations for the Supreme Being:

The Ashanti conception of the Supreme Being may be gathered from the titles ascribed to him. He is, the Ashanti say, older than all the things that live on the wide earth (Asase tere, na Onyame ne Panin). He is Onyankopon, Alone the Great One; Tweaduampon, the Dependable One; Bore, the First, the Creator of all things; Otumfo, the Powerful One; Odomankoma, the Eternal One.[20]

There is a myth which is known by most people among the Akans. This has formed part of the oral tradition as Busia relates:

According to a well-known myth, Onyankopon long, long ago lived very near to men. His abode was the sky. There was a certain old woman who used to pound her fufu (a meal of mashed yam or plantain) and whenever she did so, the long pestle she used knocked against Onyankopon who lived just above in the sky. So one day Onyankopon said, 'Because of what you have been doing to me, I am taking myself away far up into the sky where men cannot reach me.' So he went up and up into the sky, and men could no longer approach him ... As the myth ... proves, the Ashanti have for a long time held the belief that the Supreme Being has removed himself too far for man to approach directly and can only be approached through intermediary deities.[21]

We can conclude by saying that in all matters of immediate concern, the African is interested in the ancestral spirits, but believes that the Supreme Being is Omnipotent. Religion in Africa is like any other religion and deals with the same spiritual matters. The content is the same but the procedures may vary according to the social development of the people.

REFERENCES

1 Recent works of African religion show evidence of a reorientation in the right direction. See, for example, *African Systems of*

Thought, M. Fortes and G. Dieterlen, (eds.), London: Oxford University Press, 1965, and Michael Banton (ed.), 1966.

2 E. E. Evans-Pritchard, *Theories of Primitive Religion*, London: Oxford University Press, 1965, pp. 6-7.

3 E. O. James, *The Concept of Deity*, Hutchinson's University Library, 1950, p. 31.

4 James, 1950.

5 Piddington, 1950, p. 359.

6 Mair, 1964, p. 189.

7 Nicholas S. Timasheff, *Sociological Theory: Its Nature and Growth*, New York, Random House 1957. Revised edition, p. 112.

8 Timasheff, 1957, p. 112, para. 3.

9 It would be just as absurd to try to draw a comparison between Roman Catholic and Protestant beliefs by witnessing their respective religious services.

10 Evans-Pritchard, 1965, p. 79.

11 Morris Ginsberg, 'Foreword' to Hobhouse, p. xxiii.

12 Busia, 'The Ashanti' in *African Worlds*, C. D. Forde (ed.), London: Oxford University Press, 1954, p. 193.

13 Guthrie as quoted by M. Fortes and G. Dierterlen, 'Preface' to *African Systems of Thought*: Studies presented and discussed at the Third International African Seminar in Salisbury, Rhodesia, 1960.

14 Radcliffe-Brown, 1952, p. 163.

15 Busia, 1954, p. 191.

16 Fortes and Dieterlen, 1965.

17 Busia, 1954, p. 191.

18 W. E. Abraham, *The Mind of Africa*, London: Weidenfeld and Nicolson, 1962, p. 51.

19 Abraham, 1962, p. 52.

20 Busia, 1954, p. 192.

21 Busia, 1954, p. 192.

XI

Festivals

FESTIVALS ARE common to all human societies. They are the only means apart from worship whereby man has sought from time immemorial, to express his awareness of a transcendental being outside himself. Man has always believed that there are certain cosmic forces which manifest themselves in deities, gods in material form, or a God. These deities or supernatural beings are said to control the world through certain ineluctable laws, the infractions of which could cause misfortune. They are also believed to have feelings and senses similar to those of human beings and they react to stimuli in the same way as man. Festivals combine economic and religious activities, for they are observed with material things. Food and animals constitute the main instruments of festivals. Animals are slaughtered and sometimes food is offered to gods. There are many festivals among most African societies. These festivals vary according to the ecology and the social structure of the people. I take my examples from Ghana from the ethnic group known as Akans. The Akans are the largest ethnic groups with distinct cultural and linguistic similarities. The Akans inhabit most of the forest areas, and they are mostly sedentary farmers and fishermen. They depend on nature for their livelihood. Their cosmological ideas are linked to their fishing and farming habits. In this way they have several festivals which express their dependence on nature. The Akans are matrilineal societies by definition. I describe four major types of festivals common to the Akans. These are Adaes, of which Awukudae falls on Wednesdays, and Akwasidae falls on Sundays; Ohum festivals, of two types, the main one for elders and the minor for the general public, known as the 'mmarante Ohum' or the 'festival for the young men or the young'; fertility festivals which are the first-fruit festivals for the gods; Odwira festivals which are for the ancestral spirits.

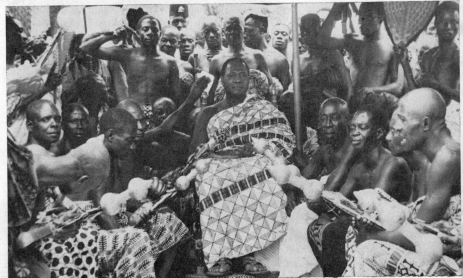

Left, three Ga girls, who have gone through the initiation rites. *Below,* the installation of the present Asantehene, Opoku Ware II, October 1970.

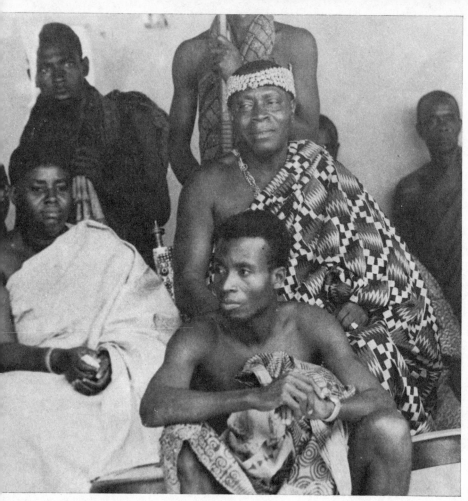

Above, Akwamu Nana Akoto
II celebrating an Adae Festival.
Left, the Afutu deer hunt.

The two pictures on the left show a girl carrying water for her ancestral spirits en route to Nsorem. She is in a trance—indicative of the fact that the spirits have descended to drink the water. *Above*, the wife of the paramount chief carrying a receptacle containing food for the royal ancestors en route to the royal mausoleum. She is at the rear of the procession.

Left, Adumhene, chief of the executioners, going with the procession. A section of the procession (*above*) showing elders connected with the stool house assisting one of the carriers of the food for the royal ancestral spirits. The picture below shows elders of a royal lineage in the procession with a woman carrying a brass container with food for their ancestral spirits.

There are two forms of Adae. These are Awukudae and Akwasidae, respectively. Adae is an important rite performed by chiefs and elders of the clan and lineages. They are also used as units for counting the days and months of the year. They mark out the seasons, and indicate the kinds of agricultural activities that should be undertaken at each particular season. Every Akwasidae consists of two clear weeks and five days, and each Awukudae consists of forty days (40). This means that every two weeks and three days after is an Akwasidae and every two weeks and four days after it another Akwasidae. The Friday preceding ten days to Akwasidae is called 'Fofie' meaning 'Friday' or ritual Friday. The Tuesday, which precedes nine days to Awukudae is 'Kwabena'. The Saturday which comes before Awukudae is called 'Memeneda Dapaa' and the Tuesday is called 'Beneda Dapaa'. On every 'Dapaa' day the chief's drummers herald its coming in the evening before by drumming. This act of drumming is called 'Dapaatu' meaning the ritual heralding of the Adae.[1]

The Akans have three hundred and sixty days in the year according to this reckoning and not three hundred and sixty-five days. The main function of the Adae festivals is ritual. On Adae days the chief with the help of his special stool-functionaries ritually purifies his soul. This idea is consistent with the concept of divine kingship. The chief's soul is sacrosanct and so is his body. He is therefore preserved by special rites on such festive occasions. Adae is also a day of rest like the Jewish Sabbath, it starts at sunset the previous day with drumming, and the day is dominated by feasting and drinking.

Akwasidae is an important festival among the Ashantis, who do not observe the Odwira Festival, which is a special festival for the commemoration of all important ancestors. The Adae festivals and the Odwira Festival constitute one generic ancestor worship, for the festivals are meant for the ancestral spirits and they are calendrical and commemorative. Odwira festivals are observed by the Akans found in the south-eastern part of Ghana, the Akwapim and Akwamus. The Odwira festival combines a first-fruit festival and ancestral worship. The social and political significance of the Odwira festival is affirmed by the collaboration of all the other chiefs in the area. Fortes's analysis of the 'clanship and ritual collaboration' among the Tallensi fits the Akan situation, in that the Odwira festival is observed by the Akwamus and Akwapim, and the Akwasidae observed by the Ashantis and other tribes show how 'social ties and cleavages are most conspicuously affirmed' in these societies..' and how 'Ritual collaboration and common ritual allegiances are indices of common interests and mechanisms of solidarity.'[2] While the Earth cults, according to Fortes, are locally collective ritual celebrations, and sometimes may encompass a collection of various lineages and clans, the External Boyar or shrine may attract many worshippers from several tribes, thus mirroring and confirming the social solidarity of a wide area of diverse tribal units who may have common interests in certain things but differ and may even be mutually or diametrically opposed to one another in restricted inter-tribal and parochial matters. These Boyar celebrations serve as a mechanism for the interplay of fission and fusion within the society. The Adaes which occur at fixed times of the year are local festivals among the various tribes which celebrate the Odwira Festival at the appropriate time, but the Odwira Festival is regarded as a national affair.

Besides being a national festival it is also a calendrical festival because it occurs annually like the Christmas season. Odwira is the culmination of all the seven preceding Adaes, the Adae festivals which occur at forty-day intervals. This makes the African year a little less than three hundred and sixty-five days.

ODWIRA FESTIVAL

Every eight Awukudaes marks the beginning of ritual preparation for the Odwira Festival and it is referred to 'Adae Butu'. This then is the ritual period treated like Lent. The period covers six weeks and it is rigidly observed. A ban is placed on all social activities including funeral rites. On the last Wednesday of the six ritual weeks all elders who possess blackened stools in their lineage get ready to give the ancestors food. The Wednesday is a day of mourning. All the people who die during the ritual preparation week and others who have died before are remembered. There is

plenty of drinking, wailing and the singing of traditional mourning and war songs depending on the rank of the person being remembered. If the person is a high ranking chief or elder, talking
drums are played. On the following Thursday, every elder gives
symbolic food or administers what to all intents and purposes is a
sacramental supper. The Chief goes to the stool repository, and
with the ritual stool-functionaries he goes through a special rite,
re-affirming his allegiance to his ancestors. This esoteric ritual is
performed by the chief carrying a sheep on his shoulders, with a
piece of cloth round his waist, bare-foot, while the stool father
pours a libation to the ancestral spirits, both previous occupants of
the various stools and members of the royal lineage who are dead.
At the conclusion of the libation the sheep is placed before the stools
and slaughtered and the blood is used for besmearing the stools by
the stool carriers. On the same day, the chief and other minor
chiefs and some of the lineage heads visit the mausoleum, which
is visited only once a year when the path to it is cleared. The
mausoleum is called 'Nsorem', and on the afternoon of the Thursday the chief, that is, the paramount chief or divisional chief,
prepares food called 'oto', mashed yam mixed with egg and
seasoned with palm oil; neither salt nor pepper is put into this
because it is believed that spirits do not eat salt or pepper. The chief
proceeds with all the minor chiefs who have also prepared some
food, and the food is carried on earthen receptacles by virgin girls,
to the 'nsorem' for the ancestral spirits. Some of the food is placed
on the blackened stools at each chief's or lineage head's stool at
the stool repository before going to the mausoleum. Later other
minor rites are performed. On the Friday a durbar is held and all
the chiefs and sub-chiefs meet to affirm or re-affirm allegiances.

ABOAKYIR FESTIVAL IN THE AFUTU STATE

Aboakyir is a special festival observed by the Afutus, who are part
of the common linguistic stock of the tribes called the Akans. They
resemble the Guans of the Akwapim ridge in some of their dialectical constructions. Aboakyir is historically similar to the Jewish
Passover. It is based on a certain historical incident. The validating
myth is contained in a short historical statement concerning the
journey and the arrival of the Afutus in their present habitat. It

also tells of the safe conduct and protection given to their ancestors by their god, Penkye Otu. The Afutu are said to have travelled eastwards from an unnamed place near Cape Coast to their present home. 'Tradition says this festival is more than 300 years old and dates from the time that the Afutu first settled at their present home'.[3]

It is believed that this tribal god demanded an annual human sacrifice from the people, and the person to be sacrificed should be a member of the royal family. This practice went on for a few years, but its continuance constituted a serious threat of extermination of all the strong members of the royal family; the Afutu therefore substituted a leopard which was to be caught alive with bare hands annually. This hunting expedition was bedevilled with many fatal hazards and resulted in even greater loss of life, so they consulted their god again and pleaded with him to allow them to substitute deer blood because the blood of a deer was said to be nearest to human blood. The deer hunting (Owasang) occurs about Easter time; on the Sunday after each deer hunt, the chief priestess of the shrine of Penkye Otu, begins to count the days to the next festival. Unlike the Akans who mark the calendrical time-space by various Adae festivals, the Afutus express the time-space by this special rite performed by the chief priestess. She puts a roll of a chewing sponge called 'sawee' in a special receptacle, repeating this rite every succeeding fourth Sunday. After she has placed the eleventh ball, this coincides with Easter-tide. The chief priestess or the matron of the shrine informs the chief priest called Botse Komfoano. He in turn informs the paramount chief, after which he enters into ritual confinement. While the priest is going through ritual purification, the Omanhene will then summon the two principal 'military companies' called Asafo Tuafo No. 1 and Dentifo No. 2 companies. This summoning of the two principal companies signifies the approach of the deer hunting 'aboakyir'. The Captain of each company presents a demi-John (a large pot-like bottle) of wine to the Tufuhene, who in order of political ranking is the deputy paramount chief. The Tufuhene shares the drink among the two companies. This signifies the ritual fixing of the date for the festival. After these preliminary ritual overtures, all the people of the state prepare themselves for the festival day which falls either in April or May. The period for preparation takes two weeks, and on the Thursday following the Monday of drinking the Company wine or 'Asafo-Nsa', the Captains of the two companies don their traditional military attire and present themselves to the paramount chief. The captains of the two main companies (Asafo) each wear different military attire befitting his military rank. The captains of No. 1 Company (Tuafo) wear short smocks and carry a cutlass, and members of their companies wear motley-coloured dresses. The captains of No. 2 Company (Dentifo) wear chain-mail, iron helmets and bear war swords. The other captain of No. 2 Company is also allowed to carry a cutlass as a mark of a special honour conferred on his ancestors by a Dutch Governor in recognition of the part played by them during a battle against the people of Elmina and neighbouring tribes of the Dutch settlers. Each military dress has some kind of historical significance, and ascriptive status. Sometimes it confers on the wearer some distinctive honour, which places him over others. On the eve of the deer hunt, an all-night vigil is kept in preparation for the great event. At this time oracles may be consulted and magical practices are revived. Each company tries to gather the necessary inspiration and assurance from both the ancestral spirits and oracles.

Early in the morning at cock-crow the two main companies and their sub-divisions assemble at the centre of the town armed with sticks and cudgels. The first to set out for the hunting expedition is the No. 1 Company. This company goes further afield to give a wide berth to the Company No. 2 which follows immediately after No. 1 Company is out of sight.

The next stage is characterized by traditional drumming in the centre of the town in the presence of the paramount chief and his councillors. All the people wait feverishly for the first company to catch the deer and bring it alive. The first to catch the deer returns to the town with great excitement and places the deer before the daïs where the paramount chief holds his ceremonial and other meetings. The chief is then informed of this catch and he hurries to the place. On arrival the chief removes the sandal from his right foot and places his bare foot three times on the panting deer, and then he turns to the victorious company and commends them for their adroitness. The company withdraws and goes home, while the chief waits patiently for the second company to return. According to tradition the chief has to wait until the last man has returned safely from the chase. If a company is unable to catch a deer then the captain presents the chief with a bottle of drink as 'a dismissal drink'. The Omanhene joins the Asafo companies and the spectators in procession with the captured deer on the shoulders of the victorious captain, and the procession makes for the Penkye Otu shrine, which is situated in the centre of the town. The captured deer is slaughtered after the chief priest has performed all the necessary rites. The paramount chief holds a durbar with all the pageantry and pomp that befits his position. The full account of the deer hunt has been described by Mr A. A. Opoku in his new book.[4] The Aboakyir festival is an annual festival, and it conforms in structure and function to other festivals, especially the Jewish Passover. It is a reminder of the protection which Penkye Otu gave the Afutu's ancestors during their wanderings. 'The Passover, Pesah bearing a two fold reminder of the advent of the springtide and the liberation of Israel from Egypt, and bright with promise of the deliverance which the future awaits Israel and all mankind'.[5] Aboakyir renews the hopes of the Afutu State, and brings the people together, thus renewing the social sentiments.[6]

REFERENCES

1 Ayisi, 1965.
2 M. Fortes, *The Dynamics of Clanship among the Tallensi*, London: 1945, p. 98.
3 cf. A. A. Opoku, 'Festivals of Ghana' State Publishing Corporation, 1970, p. 33.
4 Opoku, 1970.
5 Cf. Milton Steinberg, *Basic Judaism*, p. 131.
6 Radcliffe-Brown, 1952, p. 157. 'Rites can be seen to be the regulated symbolic expressions of certain sentiments. Rites can therefore be shown to have a specific social function when, and to the extent that they have for their effect to regulate, maintain and transmit from one generation to another sentiments on which the constitution of the society depends.'

XII

The Logic of Ritual Practices and Taboo

I HAVE already discussed special rites in connection with initiation as described by Van Gennep.[1] This refers to a specific social institution. Ritual practices are pervasive in all human societies, and in some, they are observed in the everyday life of the individual and the group from cradle to grave. For example, the grown-ups or household heads or lineage heads of the Akan tribe in Ghana are exhorted to put the first morsel of food on the ground for ancestors before eating or to pour a drop of water or drink on the ground for the ancestors; these are symbols which reaffirm the belief in the world of spirits as an integral part of cosmological belief. Though this practice may seem simple and may sometimes be regarded as sociologically dysfunctional, its metaphysical plausibility is demonstrated by the psychological value of the practice to the people.

In most primitive societies the world of the living and that of the dead are intricately and inexorably dovetailed. According to the Akan belief, death does not end kinship ties. These ties persist and lineage membership therefore includes the living and the dead. Busia is clear on this point in his book. 'But death does not sever the ties of kinship. Between the dead and the living relatives the bond of kinship is believed to persist'.[2] The dead members of the lineage influence the lives of the living and the most senior of these—that is, those who had occupied special ranks before death—constitute the ancestral spirits, and provide an important mechanism for social control.

Contact with the spiritual world, either to supplicate for beneficence, or to atone for sins committed, is established by following certain prescriptive rules. These rules are hedged about by myths in order to give them some validity and universal acceptance amongst the people. Gluckman observes that:

Among the important mechanisms of control and adjustment

in tribes are mystical beliefs of various kinds. I here follow
Evans-Pritchard who contrasted 'mystical' beliefs as occuring
in operations which are out of sensory observation and
control, with empirical beliefs which state knowledge
of operations in which every step is under sensory observation
and control'.[3]

Rituals are therefore the only means through which the profane
world is brought into contact with the sacred. They serve as institutional intermediaries or sanctifying agents. There are various
kinds of rituals. which may be simple or complex. *Simple rituals*
may take the form of pouring the first few drops of one's drink on
the ground and calling the name of one's dead father or other
relative to come and partake before drinking oneself. By this ritual
the social link between the person and the dead relative is ac-
knowledged. The pouring of drink is known as a *libation* and may
be elaborate on some occasions. If rituals are simple they do not
require a special functionary, as private prayers are distinct from
prayers which only priests may recite for baptism or marriage etc.
... I call these simple acts *personal rituals*. *Complex rituals* are
rituals which involve the participation of another person or persons other than the one performing the ritual. This may be the
ritual for supplication or prayers rendered by a household head or
a lineage head for a member of the lineage. They may be rituals
for funeral rites—or mortuary rites. These may be performed by a
senior member of the lineage because by virtue of his position in the
group he has direct access to members of the lineage in the spirit
world. These I call *group* or *social rituals* and they are also by
definition complex. One person performs the rites on behalf of the
whole group but need not have any special expertise. Most complex
rituals are formal. Formal rituals are both elaborate and complex
and are only performed by special functionaries, either medicine
men, priests or priestesses. They receive special fees in kind for
their services and they claim to possess the power of clairaudience
and clairvoyance. Rituals are the means by which the sacred and the
profane are brought together without doing damage to the social
fabric.

TABOO

The English term taboo traces its ancestry to the Polynesian term taboo which means to forbid, and it covers a wide range of prohibitions. The term has shed some of its Polynesian connotations and has found a comfortable habitat in sociology and social anthropology.

According to Sir James Frazer, who first gave the term serious sociological attention the term was imported by the voyagers who visited Polynesia—and they used the term for a special kind of prohibition which they illustrated by the physical avoidance of certain things or categories of people, such as a new-born infant, a corpse or the person of a chief—all these were said to be taboo. The physical distance which one was expected to maintain from these things was controlled by a series of sanctions which constituted an effective deterrent against possible infraction. A man who touched any of these things became taboo himself and was expected to submit himself to prescribed ritual purification. It was believed that if such ritual purification were not performed the person was exposed to danger and something unpleasant would happen to him, such as an illness, which might eventually spread to the whole community. The victim then constituted 'a sociological virus',[4] which could spread like an epidemic. The performance of purification was referred to as noa,[5] the opposite of taboo.

Frazer maintained that there was danger in using the Polynesian term without qualification, so he specified the use of the term in another social situation not comparable to the Polynesian situation but to be used as a heuristic concept. Frazer was followed by Radcliffe-Brown according to whom a ritual prohibition is a rule of behaviour which restricts the freedom of movement of a person within certain social fields vis-à-vis contact with an object or person. These rules have religious implications and people who overlook them feel a sense of guilt and seek ritual restoration. The concept of ritual prohibition presumes that the individual has a ritual value or possesses a sacred entity—which should not be allowed to come into touch with certain objects or persons. Any physical proximity produces a negative effect which deprives the individual of his ritual status and value, and the qualities which maintain his well-being are then endangered. When this happens, the individual is desecrated and he becomes a source of danger to himself and society.

Radcliffe-Brown gave two examples of these ritual prohibitions from contemporary England which he maintained essentially resembled the Polynesian examples. One was the practice which enjoins a person who spills salt to throw a pinch of the spilt salt over his shoulder to obviate bad luck. The other was the Roman Catholic practice of abstaining from eating meat on Fridays, especially during Lent, exemption from this being granted by dispensation, without which it would constitute a sin which could only be absolved by the ritual process of confession. Eating meat on Fridays therefore deprives the person who does so of his ritual status as a Catholic.

Among other examples, Radcliffe-Brown quoted the Kikuyu tribes in East Africa and their ritual prohibitions against touching or carrying a corpse, stepping over a corpse, eating food from a cracked pot, coming into contact with a woman's menstrual discharge etc. The term used to cover these prohibitions is *thahu* and it portended bad luck or misfortune which could only be obviated by a priest or a medicine-man through a prescribed ritual exercise. If an Elder with some rank or a woman when coming out of the hut slips and falls down on the ground, he or she remains motionless until someone in the neighbourhood comes and sacrifices a sheep. Among the Akans in Ghana there are certain acts which people of high social ranking should abstain from, such as eating food cooked by a woman during the entire course of her menstrual period. A chief should not see a corpse or touch one. There are several other ritual prohibitions which are essentially similar to the examples quoted above. For example a widow has to observe certain ritual prohibitions; she is expected to dramatise her loss by mourning—which implies the wearing of black cloth—fasting during the period when her husband's body lies in state or before the body is interred, refraining from normal life and suspending all social contacts for a specific period, sometimes one year. In some cases the widow is subjected to both physical and mental torture by the relatives of the late husband as a reminder of the husband's kindness to his wife and presumably a foretaste of the difficulties which the widow might experience without the husband as her companion.

The kinds of ritual prohibitions which are seen in most Polynesian societies are also found in various forms in most African societies, with a few cultural modifications. They also reflect the religious and cosmological beliefs of the society. Many such prohibitions exist but it is not necessary to cite many examples here.

I may however mention that the term taboo has now acquired other meanings in everyday usage. It may be used to express personal dislike of certain things or persons. For example the names of certain individuals are taboo—or certain places—because they have unpleasant memories for a person.

REFERENCES

1 Rite-de-passage. See p. 48, 'Mechanics of Social Adjustment'.
2 Busia, 1951, Ch. 17, para. 5.
3 M. Gluckman, *Politics, Law and Ritual in Tribal Society*, Oxford: Blackwell, 1965, p. 216.
4 This term is used heuristically—with biological implications as found in epidemiology.
5 Radcliffe-Brown, p. 133.
'In the second place he is also dangerous to other persons—he is tabu in the same sense as the thing he has touched. If he should come in contact with utensils in which or the fire at which food is cooked, the dangerous influence would be communicated to the food and so injure anyone who partook of it'.

XIII

Social Change in Africa

THEORIES OF social change are not new to social scientists. Heraclitus, the Greek thinker, developed a theory of social change, however naïve this may now appear. He expressed his views about the change which occurs in societies in rather sombre tones. His emphasis on change, particularly as it affected kings was gloomy—'kings and things change', 'everything is in flux', 'you cannot step twice into the same river'. The burden of his theory is that change necessarily ended in decay and not in progress, and this spirit was consistent with the mood of the period. I should like to turn to other less depressing theories of change.

The Comtean dynamic theory emphasized the idea of progress. The paradigm was essentially evolutionary and in this way also Comte was reflecting the spirit of his era (early nineteenth century France). He saw society as a natural organism with the progressive development of human knowledge from the lowest level, called theological or fictive, to metaphysical or philosophical, and thence to the scientific or positive stage. Comte was obviously anti-clerical and he directed his critique against Catholicism with all its excesses in society. He advocated a new social order with increasing liberalization of human sentiment and the prevalence of a new ethic which he called 'altruism'. Society according to this doctrine would be free of its superstitious encumbrances and science would be the key to human knowledge. The weakness of this theory is now evident, but at the time it seemed a useful working hypothesis.

Emile Durkheim, who followed Comte, studied changes occurring in law and distinguished and described two types of societies —one characterized by organic solidarity and the other by mechanical solidarity. Law in the mechanical society was repressive because in this society the collective conscience was said to be strong. In the next stage the society was characterized by organic solidarity and the law in this society is said to be contractual, based on the division of labour and interdependence; the collective conscience is mentioned at this stage. Here Durkheim pushed his analysis too far but that was the way of all evolutionary theorists. At least this theory and Comte's were an improvement on Heraclitus's theory, for they attempted to demonstrate an upward movement of societies from simple to complex.

Max Weber's concept of 'the history of social change as a process of increasing rationality or the rejection of magical ideas as the understanding of the world increases [the disenchantment of society] is one that many social anthropologists have found illuminating'.[1] He also sees a change in the composition of social groupings—a change from primary, face-to-face or Gemeinschaft groups to Gesellschaft secondary groupings (This dichotomy originated with another German thinker, F. Toennies). Weber's contribution to the theory of social change demonstrates dynamic theory working in many examples and shows how tension between tradition and innovation produces enduring change. Thus tension between traditional leadership and charismatically dominated leadership produces legal-rational leadership.

Finally we come to Karl Marx. Marx's dynamic theory of change is revolutionary. It attempts to demonstrate the historical development from primitive through feudal to industrial societies and predicts a socialist and communist type as the end-product. The dialectic of his analysis is rigorous and categorical. His theory of change is based on conflict theory. As Firth observes:

> Dahrendorf has pointed out one of Marx's greatest contributions to social theory was his success in tracing conflicts that effect social change back to the patterns of social structure. For Marx, special conflicts were not random occurrences which forbid explanation and hence prediction, but were the specific outgrowths of the structure of society. While mistaken in his view that the only way in which social conflict could produce structural change was by revolutionary upheaval, Marx nevertheless in his use of a variant of Hegelian dialectic did focus attention on the significance of looking for the seeds of change in apparently stable forms under scrutiny'.[2]

This, then, in my view is the main basis of the Marxian conflict theory of change or what is sometimes described as the materialistic interpretation of history.

Although Marx has laid himself open to mixed reactions to his theory of change many writers have found some elements of his ideas useful for further sociological investigation, particularly the economic factor of social change. The greatest contribution Marx made to sociological theory was his emphasis on change in the infrastructure as a prerequisite for his Utopian society of classlessness. The monocausal aspect of this theory unfortunately provoked the excessive strictures which have overshadowed its value. The assumption contained in the theory is valid in many respects as events have proved in modern times.

The term social change, by general agreement among sociologists, refers to the changes which occur in the social structure of societies. It presupposes an evolutionary process, a change from a simple stage to a complex and better stage, an upward movement process. It further presupposes progress, thus giving this phenomenon, almost a teleological twist. But a change may either be an improvement of a *status quo*, or a retrogression to the *ante status quo*. It may even show signs of social pathology. Thus change in the Roman Empire meant decadence in its imperial influence and a change in the British Empire meant a diminution of British influence and the curtailment of her maritime power.

But social change in Africa has meant progress in some parts and abject negation of self-determination in other parts. For example, in Southern Rhodesia and South Africa, civil liberty has ceased to be enjoyed by the natives and appropriated exclusively by the minority of white settlers. In West Africa social change has brought a degree of independence for the indigenous sons of the respective countries —freedom from external domination—but seems to have resulted in elected authoritarian governments. Africa cannot be juxtaposed along with Europe in terms of sociological analysis, because Africa has not experienced the violent shocks which convulsed the social systems of pre-industrial Europe, particularly English Society in the 18th Century. The changes which have so far occurred in Africa have not caused any radical change in the social fabric. This is because of the peculiar and resilient structure of African societies, which is amenable to change. In discussing change in Africa, however, we have to take into account certain variant features of the societies because Africa has undergone a process of Westernization. When the Western powers shared the continent amongst themselves, the Colonial powers adopted different types of administration and these have influenced the people in different ways. Both Drs Wilfred Cartey and Martin Wilson state the case cogently.

'The manner in which African societies adapted to European colonial rule from the turn of the twentieth century onward depended in large part on the policy of administrative and political overrule employed by European powers. There were, in general, two types of policies of colonial administration established in African colonies. One, utilized by the French, Belgians and Portuguese, is known as Direct Rule; the other, utilized by the British, is called Indirect Rule'.[3]

These various colonial experiences have affected the political development of the peoples of Africa. French Colonial policy aimed at the fraternization of certain individuals of their dependent countries who had reached certain cultural levels (i.e. black Frenchmen), and gave them equal political status. This was known as the principle of assimilation. Here Wellerstein's analysis is pungent.

This then, is the classic contrast between Africa's two colonial powers, Britain and France; Britain—Empirical, commercial, practicing indirect rule, keeping Africans at a distance, verging on racism; France—Cartesian in its logic, seeking glory, practicing direct administration, acting as apostle of fraternity and anti-racism. Anyone who travels in both British and French Africa will see the grain of truth in these generalizations. The flavour of life is different; the two colonial powers have produced two different cultures. And yet, anyone who travels there well knows the severe limitations of these generalizations.[4]

These colonial policies had their negative aspects but they also contained certain positive and good elements. Almost everywhere in Africa, there were systems of tribal groupings to facilitate administrative procedures. These groupings promoted tribal integration which welded the people together and prepared the way for national consciousness during the nationalist agitations for independence. Sometimes certain African nationalists have accused former colonial masters of breaking up Africa into little groups and so dividing the Continent by artificial national boundaries in order to perpetuate their rule. This of course is mere chauvinism and does not bear out the true facts of the history of Africa. Africa was never culturally homogeneous, and each country had small autonomous ethnic groups. The revolution in communications introduced by the former Colonial powers accelerated cultural and tribal assimilation. I do not subscribe to a naïve generalization about the unique civilization of the African past, though, I do share in the idea of Africa's rich cultural heritage. Here I give Nkrumah's argument when he was commenting on 'African Socialism':

'Today, the phrase "African Socialism" seems to espouse the view that the traditional African society was a classless society imbued with the spirit of humanism and to express a nostalgia for that spirit. Such a conception of socialism makes a fetish of the communal African society. But an idyllic, African classless society (in which there were no rich and no poor) enjoying a drugged serenity is certainly a facile simplification; there is no historical or even anthropological evidence for any such a society. I am afraid the realities of African society were somewhat more sordid. All available evidence from the history of Africa up to the eve of the European colonization, shows that African society was neither classless nor devoid of a social hierarchy.'[5]

Any attempt to examine social change in Africa may lead inevitably to certain general assumptions which may not be valid for Africa as a whole, because of the differences in the respective colonial administrations. But certain features of change may be amenable to common theoretical analysis, and may therefore be brought under these assumptions with qualified provisos.

THE EFFORTS OF THE EARLY ANTHROPOLOGISTS

The early anthropologists who were concerned with the study of non-industrial or preliterate cultures, were preoccupied with the analysis of social structures. They saw human societies as made up of structures, or tangible layers which could lend themselves to empirical analysis, and could even be isolated for comparison in order to provide a meaningful analysis of the whole social system. These anthropologists attempted 'holistic studies' of these societies, treating African peoples as 'a human type'. They hazarded certain hypotheses which classified Africans as 'primitive' racial groups, homogeneous in social development. It was contended by these writers that the nature of such societies rendered them resistant to civilization in the Western sense.

This is not surprising, because these anthropologists were studying cultures with which they were not familiar, and they therefore lacked the intellectual equipment to see beneath the symbolic expressions, customary nuances, and emotional proclivities of these peoples. The best they could achieve in the face of these bewildering difficulties was to construct artificial models, categories, and distinctions and sometimes identifications which did not reflect the true nature of the social complexities. Nowadays, intensive research into African societies and accumulated, well-documented material has thrown a flood of light on these cultures and much steady progress is being made in our understanding of these cultures. But we are still treading on slippery ground in some areas of investigation, as pointed out by an eminent anthropologist, Jack Goody:

> The major problems that face the comparative study of human society especially as concerns simple societies are two-fold. The first has to do with the reliability of its observations. Accounts of overt ritual activities present relatively few difficulties. Some aspects of social life such as divorce, residence and similar features are being subjected to crude numerical treatment. It is rather in the spheres of 'norms' and 'concepts' where field workers often seem to lose sight of the criteria of evidence of the differences between assertions and

demarcation or indeed of any idea that replicability (or the possibility of replicability) is desirable.[6]

Goody touched the crux of the whole problem in the modern trend of social anthropology. The discipline has or should necessarily undergo a change because the subject matter is changed. The rate of change is such that areas which were regarded as examples of primitiveness have now changed overnight and bear many marks of modernity. The people have also changed; many of them are at the hub of national affairs in their respective countries. For example Fortes's Tallensi in Northern Ghana can no longer be described as an acephalous society, for this area now has a representative in the National Assembly. The study of social change will mainly increase our knowledge of the agents of change.

We may distinguish two types of change in every society, namely structural and organizational change.

Structural change refers to the change which occurs in the various components of the social system, such as the contraction in the family size and kinship affiliations. This change may express itself in the area within which social responsibility is obligatory, and corporate feelings are effective. The nuclear family becomes the ideal-type of family unit towards which every person aspires. Change takes place in the marital status of women, and the new roles which they play as their status changes. These various changes are reflected in budgetary arrangements and financial responsibility is shared between spouses proportionately according to a partner's financial capacity and profession.

Organizational change refers to the new way of doing things. This is reflected in the economic sphere as well as the technological sphere. The major changes may be classified as follows: (a) economic change (b) religious change (c) political change.

ECONOMIC CHANGE

In the area of economic change there has been a definite shift from subsistence local-sufficiency-economy to world-economy. The traditional economy was largely subsistence agriculture, or pastoralism, or a mixture of both, with side-lines of simple crafts. Each village produced everything it needed, the only exception to this local sufficiency was the trade in ivory and slaves. Slaves and ivory were exported and cloth-beads, and muzzle-loading guns, were imported. In Ashanti, Ghana, flint guns were the chief imports while slaves were the main exports. There was no need for elaborate means of transport because apart from nomadic pastoralists people remained in one topographical area until calamities such as war or fire forced them to move to new areas. Even nomads whose lives were closely tied up with the exigencies of the weather changed their habitation within a narrow radius (between high and low lands). The only means of transport were mules and dug-out canoes. But nowadays Africa has been drawn into the world economic system, forming an important area of international trade. European industries derive much of their raw material from Africa. Gold, copper, vanadium, zinc, lead, tobacco, beeswax, timber, cotton and tea, are exported from all parts of Africa, and Africa in turn provides markets for the products manufactured in European countries. Africa has for a long time remained the rich market of the European countries, unable to use her raw materials for lack of capital and expertise; consequently these materials are exported to Europe, treated and refined, then re-exported to Africa.

There is now a piecemeal industrialization taking place in Africa. In Ghana, the hydroelectric power at Akosombo, provides opportunities for industrialization and already there are a few light industries. The Volta Aluminium Company (VALCO), owned partly by the Government and partly by American industrialists, who provide about 50 per cent of the capital in plant and also technical know-how, shows in microcosm the impact of economic change. The economy has been changed from subsistence to cash crop; and these economic changes have affected family and religion. Barbara Ward has observed that economic factors have exacerbated family and lineage tensions and witchcraft accusations have been on the increase with the necessary setting up of new cults to combat witchcraft machinations.[7]

Even Polly Hill maintains there have been significant changes in land distribution. In her book, *Migrant Cocoa Farmers of Southern Ghana*, she tries to show how lineage ties in turn influence the structure of land tenure—the land being divided into parallel strips for patrilineal groups and on a mosaic pattern for matrilineal groups. I am not sure if I agree wholly with this thesis, but there may be cases in which it is valid. In its general applicability to land-tenure, I doubt if it would stand scrutiny.

Akwapim, where I did my field research, seems to me to be a pertinent example of the economic factor in social change. The Akwapim are a congery of three ethnic groups who occupy an area in Southern Ghana. To the south-west, they extend as far as Berekuso, which is the westernmost Akwapim town. To the north-west, Akwapim shares a common boundary with Yilo Krobos, with the main Akwapim ridges providing a natural frontier. To the north-west, the boundary reaches the border town of Mangoase; in the south-west are Nkyenekyene, Ahamahama and Parekro. Asuoyaa and Konko are notable marginal settlements in the north-western section. Akwapim as it stands, has a total area of fifty square miles. The population of Akwapim traditional area was put at 144,790 by the 1960 population census report. Out of this number 36,250 are classified as 'Urban Dwellers' and 108,542 are 'Rural Dwellers'.

The people of Akwapim used to engage in subsistence farming—the household being the unit of production and consumption. They were, however, engaged in a cash economy on a very small scale producing palm oil. But the crop which changed the economic system was cocoa, which was brought to the district by Tetteh Quashie, a Ga blacksmith, in 1879. Tetteh Quashie came from Christiansborg, but went to Fernando Po as a casual labourer and when he was returning brought a few cocoa pods back to Mampong, Akwapim, where he was working. He established a cocoa nursery in Mampong, which turned out to be a profitable economic proposition. It is believed that the Basel Missionaries introduced some of the cocoa seedlings to Akropong, Akwapim. Polly Hill writes:

Cardinal notes that in 1856, 'The Mission were farming an agricultural station at Akropong, growing chiefly coffee and fruits as well as experimenting with grasses for thatching'. According to Wanner, Johannes Haas was the first missionary appointed as 'agricultural officer' there and in the autumn of 1857 he received some cocoa seeds from Surinam, the seedlings

from which died in 1858. Johan Jakob Lang took over the
agricultural experiments from Haas in 1858 and obtained more
cocoa seeds from another Basel Missionary, Auer, who had
brought them from Cape Palmas. In November 1861 Lang
reported that he had then got ten little cocoa trees.[8]

From the above we may infer that there was a joint effort between
the missionaries and Tetteh Quashie in the introduction of cocoa
to the area.

Cocoa, therefore, is not a natural crop in Ghana, and its introduction set in motion many changes affecting the social structure
with corresponding changes in the economic organization. It is
cultivated on a plantation basis, and it takes about six to eight
years for the trees to bear fruit. It also grows in humid areas with
plenty of rainfall and this accounts for the fact that many cocoa
farms are found in the forest regions of Ghana around Akim-
Abuakwa, Ashanti and the central parts of the country. The amount
of labour involved in cocoa cultivation is more than the household
can cope with, and this led to the hiring of outside labour for farming for the first time in Ghana. Thus changes were introduced in
the type of labour and the method of recruiting labour.

Meyer Fortes has observed in the foreword to Polly Hill's book:

For my part ... the special distinction of Miss Hill's book lies
in observations that could not have been anticipated by her, but
which represent a major contribution to the anthropological
study of West African social structures. The novelty of these
findings is the more striking to me when I compare them with
my own field observations in the cocoa-growing districts of
Ashanti in 1945-46. There, migrant farmers established themselves individually in new cocoa areas assisted only by immediate
family members. They held their land on usufructuary tenure
in virtue of an annual payment to the local chief which was
more in the nature of an acknowledgement of his chiefdom's
inalienable over-right to the land than an economic rent ...
This is very different from the group migrations described by
Miss Hill, quite astonishingly so in the case of the 'company'
system. Miss Hill shows that two forms of group organization
were followed by the migrant farmers, though their economic

aims and activities were the same. One type was (and is) invariably made up of a group of matrilineal kin, both male and female, acting as a corporate group under the leadership of a senior male who is often also the chief financier of the enterprise. The block of land purchased by the group was and remains corporately owned, but it was (and still is) farmed by the members severally in irregular parcels distributed patchwork-wise ...[9]

Both Fortes' field experience and Miss Hill's show that cocoa cultivation introduced a complex form of unit of production and sometimes the 'company' system might even embrace friends—not kinfolk. We now meet a situation in which farmers cultivated land outside their lineage land. They also employed labour on a hired basis—sometimes on the *abusa* or tripartite basis (one-third of the proceeds going to the labourer; two-thirds to the owner). Since cocoa is an export crop and it also takes many years to fructify, farmers who were engaged in cocoa farming carried on market-gardening for food and money simultaneously. Some of the people not engaged in cocoa cultivation continued with traditional farming on a much bigger scale. They sold in the towns. The export of cocoa created markets, improved communications and stimulated all kinds of economic activities. The boom period in 1920 created artificial prosperity in the country. Many things were sold in these markets including local and imported goods.

Miss Barbara Ward observes in her article:

In return for their cocoa, Ashanti hope to satisfy their ever expanding wants—for kerosene, tinned foodstuffs of all kinds, cloth, tools, cosmetics, furniture, bicycles, cars, in fact for all kinds of manufactured goods and services such as broadcasting, train, lorry and taxi transport (an article in *The Times* in 1950 stated that there were then more than 500 licenced taxis in Kumasi), for medical services and, above all, for schools. The 1920's and the post war years were boom periods; in the 1930's the price of cocoa was halved and then dropped even lower; and during the war imports were drastically restricted. After the war prices rose again and remained high, but disease threatened the trees and the only cure then known, which was cutting out, appeared to most of the farmers as an even greater threat, while, at the time of rising prices, the Government setting up of a Cocoa Marketing Board which fixed the price to be paid to the growers each year, was looked upon with very considerable mistrust.

Cocoa then, brought a very marked acceleration of economic change and greater dependence upon forces over which the Ashanti themselves had no control, and indeed of the nature of which they were entirely ignorant.[10]

The relevance of this quotation is in the fact that these economic and technological changes affected not only the kinship system, but the system of government. As the revenue from cocoa increased, so did the rate of change increase. Education opened up new horizons for the young and a keen desire to manage their own affairs was unleashed. Cocoa lifted the economy from a village subsistence economy to a national and international level. The economy of the country became linked with the world economy, so that if the price of cocoa was depressed in America or England, it affected the price of cocoa here in the country—with the corresponding result of low standards of living and unemployment.

Cocoa, then, brought many changes in Ghana, but it all started in Mampong Akwapim. What I have done in this chapter is to show how one factor can affect a whole social structure. I am not saying that there have not been other factors. A monocausal theory cannot handle social change in its entirety. Up and down the country there are small businesses, such as the Baah Company, dealing in cannery and distribution of consumer goods. In the fishing industries, motorized vessels for deep-ocean fishing have been introduced, owned by indigenous entrepreneurs. The policy of the present government is to encourage this trend of indigenous entrepreneurial participation in the private sector of the economy. In East and Central Africa, there is a definite move towards the rational distribution of land, and this has caused mass-migration of most of the white land-owners. In all, Africa has now woken up to the fact that political self-determination without economic realism will not take her an inch further towards progress. To recapitulate, the following points emerge:

(1) A shift from subsistence economy to cash economy.
(2) A change from primitive collectivism to individualism.
(3) Increased social mobility with a resultant meritocratic criteria for social ranking.

One thing is clear from the above, that in many developing countries most of the changes which have occurred were largely caused by economic factors. It is true that external factors such as colonial pressures, Christianity and education have played important roles in acculturation. But this could not have been easily brought about without the economic potential in the countries concerned. Such changes may be caused by the discovery of certain mineral deposits—a natural attraction—strategic locations, the cultivation of special crops, or natural vegetable resources such as timber. In Ghana, the changes brought about by cocoa cultivation spell out the impact of the economic factor.

RELIGIOUS CHANGE

Christianity was always identified with the flag, because the missionaries at first needed protection from the traders, and latterly, from the metropolitan powers. This alliance between the Church and the Colonial administration generated a latent suspicion which was played upon by nationalists, of the European holding a Bible in one hand, and a gun in the other. Missionary work started along the West Coast among the traders who settled along the Coast and were mostly Christians and therefore needed priests to assume spiritual oversight. It had become the accepted practice for the traders to have amongst them a handful of medical men and priests to look after the traders. Malaria was the scourge of the Guinea Coast and many of the traders were victims of malaria a few days after they landed.

It was not easy to get candidates for the Chaplaincy because of the uncertainties that accompanied life on the Coast. For a long period therefore, the small congregation which grew up was without a priest. This lack of men to look after the congregation made religious life rather sluggish, and Christian witness ineffective in the small trading community at Christiansborg. About 1829, the question of a Chaplaincy was given a degree of priority by the

Danish Government. The Company at home was becoming restive about reports of the reckless life of the traders on the Coast, so, on the recommendation of the Bishop of Zealand, certain young men offered themselves for service on the Coast ... These were young men who had not done well in their studies, the flotsam and jetsam of the Danish theological institutions, in other words the 'drop-outs'.[11] In Dr Debrunner's words the priests 'were mentally unbalanced men', 'lazy fellows', 'drunkards', and 'even crooks'.[12] This was how Christianity was seen practised by the chaplains who were sent out to Christiansborg. It is therefore not surprising that they did not make any impact on the natives. They had nothing to offer the natives. But in the central part, it started as an African adventure and the life of the English chaplains were exemplary.

'The greatest opportunity, as well as the fiercest challenge, lay in the Gold Coast. A fort was built on Cape Coast in 1651, and at varying intervals, chaplains had been appointed. In 1830, although there had been no chaplain at Cape Coast Castle for many years, a group of young Africans gathered for fellowship, Bible-reading, and prayer. One day, when they found the supply of Bibles was inadequate, they asked a Bristol merchant Captain Potter, to purchase some more for them, and he little knowing the result of his suggestion, proposed that they should also ask for the appointment of a missionary. The Governor of the settlement approved of the plan, and on his recommendation, application was made to the Wesleyan Conference. Captain Potter offered a free passage to the man appointed as his share in the venture. Joseph Dunwell was the Society's choice and Captain Potter fulfilled his promise. But a greater figure was soon to be brought by Dunwell himself.[13]

Though the missionaries had a strong and zealous ambition to bring the good news to the natives, they lost sight of the fact that the natives were not devoid of religious experience. Africans on the whole are more religious than the Athenians. The missionaries treated the natives as *tabula rasa*, in terms of religious awareness; they misunderstood their cosmological beliefs, and condemned the religious institutions which were the symbolic and psychological expressions of their social structure and milieu. The missionaries not only denounced indigenous religion but also the Islamic religions which measured up favourably to Christianity in theological ideas other than doctrinal emphasis, and tenets. The ideas of the missionaries are aptly expressed in some of the hymns which replaced the indigenous hymns:

> From *Greenland's Icy Mountains*—Bishop Heber 1819
> V.2 What though the spicy breezes
> Blow soft o'er Ceylon's isle
> Though every prospect pleases
> And only man is vile
> In vain with lavish kindness
> The gifts of God are strown
> The heathen in his blindness
> Bows down to wood and stone.

These hymns did not arouse the intended response because the words and the music were alien to African cultures, but they reflected the missionaries' own ignorance and blindness. They had failed to grasp the symbolic significance of African practices, and though statues of Mary and her Son, and Crosses in the traditional Roman Catholic churches were treated with due reverence, everything about African religious culture was regarded as pagan and idolatrous, epitomizing the devil.

The missionaries set themselves the task of converting the natives to their new religion, by direct evangelization. During this period they went into the field themselves, risking their lives, facing violent native resistance, and the vagaries of the malaria scourge and other diseases.

A second phase was characterised by an evangelical partnership between some educated natives and the missionaries. The Basel missionaries recruited freed slaves from the West Indies to help Christianize their black brothers, while the Methodist Missionary Society sent out one man who changed the character of the missionary enterprise. The name of this man was Thomas Birch Freeman, the son of an African father and an English mother. To Thomas Birch Freeman must go the credit of the establishment of Methodism in the Gold Coast. The church was started as a small prayer group, and like a mustard seed grew into a big complex. The story of the beginning of Methodism could not be better put than in the book by Allen Birtwhistle.[14] Freeman was able to withstand the ravages of the climate because of his African blood, and also helped to dispel the belief that Christianity was a peculiarly European religion. He continued the work which had been started by a group of devout African Christians with the help of Captain Potter. Once the missionaries had got the Church established, they started to found schools for teaching the new converts to read the Bible. But besides teaching them to read the Bible, the converts were also taught other subjects, such as English and arithmetic. After a time most of the teachers and catechists were trained on the Coast. The most promising among them were sent to Europe for higher education. Besides sending some of the natives to undertake higher studies in order to return home to help with the work, the wealthy traders who had become Christians sent their children to England to study medicine or read law.

NATIONALISM AND THE CHURCH

Nationalism started within the churches. With the Calvinistic doctrine of respect for authority and belief in salvation which was evident in one's personal condition on earth, most of the converts of the Lutheran and Calvinistic persuasion endeavoured to live well and to work hard to train their children. Respect for labour and human dignity were inculcated in the doctrines of the Presbyterian Churches, while Wesleyan ideas of liberation, social equality, and justice, found expression in the beliefs of those of Methodist persuasion. The Methodists were more expressive of their convictions than the Presbyterians. This point has been stressed by the late Casely Hayford, a Gold Coast nationalist:

I now come to the greatest effort in journalism on the Gold Coast in recent times—during the closing years, that is to say, of the last decade of the last century. I refer, of course, to the Gold Coast Methodist Times which was organized, edited by that able young man, the Rev. Attoh Ahuma, then in the active ministry of the Wesleyan body on the Gold Coast. The paper was the property of that body, and Attoh Ahuma

was but their servant. But the intrepid editor did not think
it right to confine the columns of the paper to church news
and religious controversy. He saw no reason why the grievances
of the people should not be ventilated, and their temporal
amelioration enhanced in as far as it lay within the power
of the spiritual organ. At the time the young editor thus
made up his mind, Governor Maxwell preparing to bring
before the Legislative Council the now famous 'Lands Bill'.
The Gold Coast Methodist at once took up the gauntlet, and
fought like a veritable Achilles; and right loyally it was
supported by the best intellect of the land.[15]

This new intelligentsia who had learnt a great deal about what
freedom meant within the churches became deeply involved in
national politics. The churches continued to grow and involve the
natives in the work of evangelism. Now most of the churches on
the West Coast are autonomous. But there have been great changes
not only in this way but the establishment of independent churches
with no link with what may be regarded as the established
churches.[16] These churches are essentially Christian in their teach-
ings but they make use of native music and dancing. In some of
these churches certain African customs, like polygamy, are permitted. Christianity is ceasing to be a religion reflecting Western
culture rather than the universal religion that had its origins in the
Middle East or Israel.

POLITICAL CHANGE

Traditional systems of government were not elaborate, because
law and order were maintained through the normative system
which was part of the social structure. Every individual learnt
through socialization the things which he was allowed to do and
those which were taboo. The belief in ancestors played an important role in the development of personal moral awareness, and the
distinction between private and public morality was thus made
tenuous because ancestral spirits controlled the world of the living.
They bestowed beneficence on people who conducted their lives
properly and inflicted calamities on delinquent individuals.
There were various levels of social control, each level linking

up with another level either of equal authority structure, of subordinate or of super-ordinate authority structure. In this way the
system was given a hierarchical posture.

1. *The household level*—Within the household, the head, who
was usually the oldest member or the father, was responsible for
order and peace. He was also responsible for matters affecting each
member of the household in regard to any person outside the
household. Sanctions within this social group were informal and
personal, the head having an incontrovertible last word in all
matters affecting members of the household.

2. *The lineage level*—At the lineage level, social control was
exercised by the oldest person of the group in the descent line with
the concurrence of representatives of the various household heads
where these existed. The head represents the ancestral spirits and
usually serves on the chief's council or even occupies an important
office in the chiefdom. At this level, the head was the recognized
authority but his authority was precariously hedged by checks and
balances which were entrenched in customary rules, reflecting the
wishes of the ancestors and the people over whom he held this
authority. Sanctions were quasi-social.

3. *The local level*—Here the chief was the recognized authority.
He had judicial, political and social functions. His designation as
chief meant that all the people of the town owed unflinching loyalty
to him. His symbol was the black stool on which he was cere-
monially placed at the time of his enstoolment. From this local
level we come to the divisional chief and paramount chief levels,
where authority was vested in the chief and a number of his functionaries. The colonial administration did not abolish these traditional institutions but adopted them and in some cases made full
use of them for their colonial policies.

Africa has undergone various political experiences, and these
have had a far-reaching impact on the political history of the people
of this great continent. Africa was shared out by the European
Powers at the turn of the 19th century and each interest attempted
to re-organize the people of her colonial area according to specific
principles accepted by the metropolitan powers of each country.
The different European legacies constitute in a large measure the
main political framework of the political systems of modern Africa.
We therefore need to review the various colonial policies in Africa.

The British were Burkean in their attitude. The traditions of the people were to be the basis of the new régime; this meant having a mixture of foreign and indigenous cultures, and hoping that the foreign would cancel out the destructive elements of the native customs. Therefore in a paternalistic fashion a dual system was evolved—a quasi-democratic system of government for the colonial peoples with the representatives of the metropolitan powers as masters, and the colonial peoples as subject-peoples, maintaining a social distance between the Africans and the whites. This is the basis of the African adage which runs, 'A pig will always grunt even if you take it to England'. The whites everywhere regarded the natives as inferior and lacking the sense of duty and responsibility for self-determination. The outcome of this policy was the system known as indirect rule.

The French on the other hand, rather paternalistic and having a Jacobin tradition coupled with aristocratic romantic ideas adopted a principle to be known as assimilation—highly selective cultural assimilation of an élite. It was clearly never their intention to confer self-government, or any other form of political autonomy on their colonies; or to subordinate the economic and political supremacy of the predominantly white colonist to the interests of the indigenous people. The distinction between citizens and subjects and the uniformity of the legal institutions symbolized their colonial philosophy—a philosophy of metropolitan centralization frankly and nakedly in the interest of France.[17] The French though they were not like the British in the way they went about their affairs in the colonies, were not giving the native the kind of egalitarian status which in principle they advocated.

Therefore when the British colonial peoples asked for self-rule, it was a demand for a full self-determination, but when the French colonial peoples said 'Yes' to de Gaulle it was a refusal to continue with the assimilation system ... bastard citizenship of France. We now have in Africa the two major political institutions in Francophone and Anglophone areas, each reflecting the type of colonial experience that has dominated the area before independence. Most countries in Africa are either independent with the administration in the hands of a minority settler group, as in Southern Rhodesia or South Africa, or in the hands of an indigenous elected majority following the pattern of the former masters. At the moment the problem of political freedom is not yet solved in any of the newly independent countries in Africa, but in countries with settler problems, the problem is acute. Although these countries claim to be independent, the administration to all intents and purposes, is a neo-colonial system with the settlers as the masters.

The colonial administrations have left differences in attitudes to matters which require concerted efforts among the people of Africa to resolve.

The élite of the Francophone states of Africa feel differently from the élite of the Anglophone states; thus efforts to attain unanimity in political determination, are fraught with uncertainty: for the French élite think in French and the English élite think in English.

But the question may be asked: are Africans really free? If the present systems are the legacies of former colonial masters, and the validations of the systems are by reference to these foreign systems, then the change may be said to have occurred in personnel and not in the system. We still have the French system of deputies in the Francophone areas and the Whitehall parliamentary system with the American system of a ceremonial or Executive President in the Anglophone areas. We must try to evolve a system consistent with our African heritage and social structure.

REFERENCES

1 Mair, 1964, p. 24, [Brackets mine.]

2 Raymond Firth, *Essays on Social Organization and Value,* London School of Economics. Monograph, 1964, p. 24.

3 Wilfred Cartey and Martin Wilson (eds.), 'Colonial Africa' *The African Reader,* Vintage Books, September 1970, p. 73.

4 Wellerstein, 'Africa—The Politics of Independence', A Vintage Original, p. 66.

5 'Independent Africa', *The African Reader,* Cartey and Wilson (eds.), 1970, p. 202.

6 Jack Goody, *Comparative Studies in Kinship,* Routledge and Kegan Paul, 1968.

7 B. Ward, 'Some Observations on Religious Cult in Ashanti', *Africa,* Volume XXVI, January 1956, Number 1, p. 47.

8 Polly Hill, *Migrant Cocoa Farmers of Southern Ghana,* Cambridge: University Press, 1963, p. 171.

9 M. Fortes: Foreword to Hill, 1963, p. vi.

10 Ward, 1956, p. 48.

11 Ayisi, 1956, p. 304 para. 3.

12 *Kirkehistoriske* (Samlinger) 7 raekke, 4 binds 3 hefte 1962. A collection of studies in Church history. Sub-title: 'Danish Chaplains Pioneers of Church and Education in Ghana', H. W. Debrunner, p. 37.

13 C. J. Davey, *March of Methodism*, p. 55.

14 A. Birtwhistle, *Thomas Birch Freeman, A western African Pioneer*, London: The Cargate Press, 1950.

15 Cf. Cartey and Wilson (eds.), independent Africa, *The African Reader*, Vintage Books 1970, p. 17.

16 Established Churches: i.e., Presbyterian, Roman Catholic, and Methodist. The others which came later, such as the Seventh Day Adventist, Salvation Army, the Apostlic, and most of the Churches with their headquarters in either Europe or America as distinct from those indigenous churches commonly called spiritual churches or separatist movements.

17 M. Fortes 'Plural Society in Africa', *The Alfred and Winifred Horne Memorial Lecture*, 1968. South African Institute of Race Relations.

Reading List

Beattie, John, *Other Cultures: Aims, Methods, and Achievements in Social Anthropology*, London: Cohen and West, 1964.

Evans-Pritchard, E. E., *Theories of Primitive Religion*, London: Oxford University Press, 1965.

Firth, Raymond (ed.), *Man and Culture: An Evaluation of the Work of Bronislav Malinowski*, London: Routledge & Kegan Paul, 1957.

Fortes, Meyer and E. E. Evans-Pritchard, *African Political Systems*, London: International African Institute, Oxford University Press, 1940.

Mair, Lucy, *An Introduction to Social Anthropology*, Oxford: Clarendon Press, 1965.

Radcliffe-Brown. A. R. and C. Daryll Forde (eds.), *African Systems of Kinship and Marriage*, London: International African Institute, Oxford University Press, 1950.

Fortes, Meyer, *Kinship and the Social Order*, Routledge & Kegan Paul, 1970.

Goody, Jack, *Comparative Studies in Kinship*, Routledge & Kegan Paul, 1968.

Glossary of Terms[1]

Affinal ties—related through marriage.

Agnates—these are kin through the father's line.

Avoidance relationships—a situation in which persons who stand in some definite relationship avoid one another formally, e.g. sons-in-law and mothers-in-law maintain asymmetrical relations, with the sons-in-law having to avoid mothers-in-law.

Clan—A unilineal descent group whose members believe that they are related to one another through descent from a common ancestor.

Classificatory terminology—a system in which lineal relatives (father, son, etc.) are addressed or spoken of by terms which apply to certain collateral relatives.

Cognates—persons descended from the same ancestor whether through males or females.

Endogamy—the rule enjoining marriage within specified social groups.

Exogamy—the rule prohibiting marriage within specified groups.

Hypergamy—marriage between a woman of low caste and a man of high caste.

Incest prohibition—prohibition of sexual intercourse between individuals related in certain degrees of kinship.

Joking relationship—a relationship in which outrageous behaviour such as insult and obscenity is permitted between two people.

Kinship—a relationship actually or putatively traced through parent-child or sibling relations and recognized for social purposes.

Lineage—A unilineal consanguineal kin group tracing descent from a known ancestor and found in two forms: patrilineage, where the relationship is traced through the males, and matrilineage where the relationship is traced through females.

Matrilineage—a matrilineage consists of all the descendants through females of a single ancestress.

Patrilineage—a patrilineage consists of all the descendants through males of a single male ancestor.

Polyandry—A form of marriage in which one woman is married to more than one man. When the men involved are brothers, the marriage is known as adelphic polyandry.

Polygamy—A general term for plural marriage including both polygyny and polyandry.

Postpartum Sex taboo—Abstention from sexual relations by a husband and wife for a year or two after childbirth.

Sibling—General term for brother and sister without specifying sex.

Sororate—The custom whereby when a woman dies the husband is expected to marry one of the sisters.

REFERENCES

1 Most of these definitions have been taken from *Notes* and *Queries in Anthropology*, London: Routledge and Kegan Paul, 1960.

Appendix

THE KOMAN or Nkoguasonfo constitute the internal structure of the paramountcy. Members of the Koman are chiefs in their own right and they form the electoral college or the king-makers.

The members are all occupants of Asona Stools (Asona is one of the seven or eight Akan clans).

They are:

1. Asonahene Odiaboo stool
2. Owereko Ampoma Stool or Abontendom stool of Aboasa
3. Obuoko Okodumase stool
4. Opanyin Kwabena Ayesu co-opted member of the Electoral College. He performs the rite which officially announces the ushering in of the Odwira festival; the rite is performed on Tuesday (Odwira Benada)
5. Akwa Gyan Twafohene stool
6. Nana Kwapong Benkum Kyeame (Spokesman for the left-wing divisional chief)
7. Nana Dokua, the Queen-mother

In addition to these seven chiefs there are other members of the paramountcy who are members of the Electoral College, but do not belong to Koman. They also occupy Asona stools.

a. Amanokromhene, Gyasehene of Akwapim
b. Mankrado of Ahwerease
c. Osomannyawa of Aburi

Some *Ibo names* and their meanings:

Sokei—Is it only the old that die.
Onwnegbuna—Please death, do not kill this child too.
Chukwuma—God knows or destines a king.

Ngozi—God's blessing is on this child.

Azikiwe—Today's generation. These days generation are prone to anger.

Onwuegbuzia—Death do not kill again.

Names of the Week—Akan Names

AKAN	MALE	FEMALE
Monday Child	Kwadwo	Adjoa
Tuesday Child	Kwanena	Abena
Wednesday Child	Kwaku	Akua
Thursday Child	Yaw	Yaa
Friday Child	Kofi	Afua
Saturday Child	Kwame	Amma
Sunday Child	Kwasi	Akosua

Among the Gas, another large ethnic group of Ghana, the naming ceremony has some detailed variations. Instead of invoking the ancestors, the master of ceremony pours water on the roof, and allows the drops to drip on the baby; then the ancestors are invoked and the name is conferred.

Index